IDEOLOGY MATTERS
China from Mao Zedong to Xi Jinping

Books by the same author

Political Philosophy of Mao Zedong
Revolutionary Violence: A Study of the Maoist Movement in India
Contemporary Indian Political Theory

Editor:

Chinese Revolution: Comparative Perspectives
Class, Caste, Gender
India Social Development Report: 2010

Coeditor:

People's Rights: Social Movements and the State in the Third World
Grass-roots Democracy in India and China
Weapon of the Oppressed: An Inventory of People's Rights in India
Land, Equity and Democracy

IDEOLOGY MATTERS
China from Mao Zedong to Xi Jinping

Manoranjan Mohanty

IDEOLOGY MATTERS: China from Mao Zedong to Xi Jinping
by Manoranjan Mohanty

First Published, 2014

ISBN 978-93-5002-265-8 (Hb)

Published by
AAKAR BOOKS
28 E Pocket IV, Mayur Vihar Phase I, Delhi 110 091
Phone : 011 2279 5505 Telefax : 011 2279 5641
info@aakarbooks.com; www.aakarbooks.com

Printed at
Saurabh Printers Pvt. Ltd., A 16, Sector IV, Noida

To

Tan Chung

(another Hunanese)

my teacher, colleague and friend

who introduced me to China Studies at Delhi University,

and arguing with whom over the past five decades at

the Institute of Chinese Studies, Delhi

has greatly influenced my thinking.

Contents

Acknowledgements

The following papers were published in the *China Report* and *Economic and Political Weekly*. I thank their editors and publishers for their consistent support over the years.

1. Mao's Portrait of Stalin
   China Report 11/4 (1975)
2. Mao, Deng and Beyond: Dialectics of Early Stage of Socialism
   China Report 20/4&5 (1984)
3. Between Truth and Revolution: Will China Opt for Detente Social Sciences?
   China Report 17/1 (1981)
4. The Political Economy of Development in PRC at 40: Socialism in the Freedom Scale
   China Report 26/1 (1990)
5. Marxism and the Chinese Practice *China Report* 21/2 (1985)
6. Power of History: Mao Zedong Thought and Deng's China
   China Report 31/1 (1995)
7. The New Ideological Banner: Deng Xiaoping Theory
   China Report 34/1 (1998)
8. Jiang Zemin's Three Represents
   Economic and Political Weekly XXVIII/14 (April 5, 2003)
9. China's Focus on Governance
   Economic and Political Weekly XXXIX/41 (October 9, 2004)
10. Hu Jintao's "Scientific Outlook on Development": CPC Grapples with the Success Trap
    Economic and Political Weekly XLII/44 (November 3, 2007)

11. Harmonious Society and Beautiful Country: Hu Jintao's Vision and the 18th Party Congress
Economic and Political Weekly XLVII/50 (December 15, 2012)
12. Xi Jinping and the "Chinese Dream"
Economic and Political Weekly XLVIII/38 (September 21, 2013)

These were put together with the help of ICS research associate Bhim Subba. I acknowledge with thanks the assistance of this promising scholar in my current research projects.

Mr K K Saxena of Aakar Books was very keen that this book came out soon as a companion volume to my *Political Philosophy of Mao Zedong*. I thank him for his initiative.

November 2013

Manoranjan Mohanty
Institute of Chinese Studies
Delhi

Preface

The ideology of the Communist Party of China has lately attracted less attention because most analysts believe that the post-Mao leadership has abandoned all ideological pretensions. It is said that China's leaders are pragmatic and they do what works. After all was it not Deng Xiaoping who said that it did not matter if the cat was black or white, if it catches mice. In this volume we present a different line of reasoning. We point out that every policy, every strategy of development has in it ideological underpinnings. It may or may not be socialist. Its ideological character may be defined in terms of known categories, their many combinations or some innovative formulation. We must understand those considerations, value preferences and order of objectives to better comprehend the policy and its practice. Ideology is a statement of ends, means and an outlook on life and all individuals, organizations and institutions have ideologies. This volume presents a discussion of ideas of Mao Zedong, an assessment of Mao by his successors, the altogether new path of development launched by Deng Xiaoping and the ideological articulations of the subsequent policies pursued by Jiang Zemin till 2002 and Hu Jintao at the 18th Congress of the CPC in 2012 and Xi Jinping's early initiatives.

Deng Xiaoping set the framework for the official approach to Mao's place in China's history. On the aftermath of the Cultural Revolution there was so much criticism of the ideological line practiced by the 'gang of four' and policies during the decade of 1966-1976 that a trend of 'de-Maoisation' was in the offing. This could have grown into the same proportion as 'deStalinisation' in the then Soviet Union under Khrushchev after the 20th Congress of CPSU in 1956. But Deng Xiaoping took the lead and the CPC Plenum in 1981 formulated a different line on Mao Zedong's role in Chinese history and Mao Zedong Thought. That it was Mao's strategic formulation on the 'New-Democratic Revolution' which successfully brought into being the People's Republic of China in 1949 was reaffirmed. At the same time, Mao's economic ideas and his role during the Cultural Revolution were criticized in no uncertain terms. This method of discriminating evaluation, as discussed in the chapter on Mao's Portrait of Stalin was pursued by Deng Xiaoping. Deng's successors stuck to that line. On the occasion of the Ninetieth Anniversary of the founding of the CPC Hu Jintao presented a glowing tribute to Mao in July 2011. In China's countryside respect for Mao had hardly waned. But in the recent years more and more memorabilia on Mao were seen all over China.

Analysing Deng Xioping's theory of 'Building Socialism with Chinese Characteristics' is another theme of this volume. If it was a simple case of adopting market economy as practiced in the western countries, there would be less difficulty for observers and policy-makers abroad to track the Chinese development experience after 1978. By now it is clear that the Chinese model crafted by Deng and evolved by the CPC under the leadership of Jiang Zemin and Hu Jintao was more complicated. It indeed had some unique features which went under the name of Chinese characteristics. What was called 'socialist market economy' meant that the state would continue to exercise its role in maintaining macro-economic coordination. While the government would actively help develop market forces, decontrol prices, provide autonomy even to the public sector units to take their own economic decisions still state planning would remain a sustained feature of the Chinese economy. Politically, the CPC-led state system was to continue as yet another feature of the market economy according to Deng for reasons of maintaining social stability and perhaps also avert a Soviet type collapse. That is why the Chinese strategy of 'reform and open door' was described as a unique historical experiment in economic development. To what extent was it building socialism and to what extent this authoritarian system generated its own contradictions are discussed in this volume.

Jiang Zemin, Deng's chosen successor, led China during a critical period from the Tiananmen Incident in 1989 till his retirement in 2002. Interpreting Deng's line and policies, implementing them to persist in the economic path of high rate of growth while institutionalising the political and economic changes, Jiang formulated important guidelines. They were finally articulated as his 'important thought of three represents'. He affirmed that the CPC must represent the primary task of developing productive forces, represent advanced culture and represent the interests of masses. There were many implications of this formulation. But two trends were legitimised by this formulation. One emphasised the need to focus on economic growth and the other opened up Party membership to the entrepreneurs. Thereafter, the Jiang Zemin line remained a reference point for the market forces in China even though there was little mention of the 'three represents' in public discourse in the succeeding decade.

The economic successes achieved under Jiang Zemin regime not only improved people's living standards and built vast urban infrastructure, it also led to the rise of China as a global power. But simultaneously, Chinese society witnessed many serious problems such as growing income inequality, regional disparities, increasing corruption and rural unrest. This was the situation which existed in China when Hu Jintao took over the Party leadership in 2002. The decade of his leadership saw several initiatives to address these problems while maintaining a reasonably high rate of growth. He propounded a 'scientific outlook on development' which called for a balanced, coordinated and comprehensive process of development. The preoccupation with growth of GDP at any cost was discouraged and the new concept emphasised growth with social justice and environmental sustainability. The charge that Hu neglected economic growth was rebutted by his supporters showing how

China became world's second largest economy in 2010 and returned to a nine per cent rate of growth in 2012 after recovering swiftly from the global economic crisis of 2008. The goal of achieving a 'well-off society' in 2020 set by Jiang Zemin was recast as 'well-off society in all respects' by Hu Jintao. Announcing the vision of building a 'harmonious society' by addressing causes of social conflict and a 'beautiful country' by promoting sound ecology Hu Jintao left his mark on the Chinese consciousness.Whether Hu's successor Xi Jinping would return to the Jiang Zemin model or continue the Hu Jintao line would be watched closely in the coming years. His slogan of fulfilling the 'Chinese dream' of 'national rejuvenation' may combine the two legacies or may lean towards one.These issues have been discussed in detail in this volume.

We need theoretical tools to analyse China's reforms and understand the governing principles underlying each phase of the policies pursued by the various regimes in China. Even when the policies are taken on their face value they are part of a pattern of initiatives. In China Mao Zedong presented a certain perspective on social transformation which was debated intensely during his lifetime and later. Deng Xiaoping inaugurated a new set of ideas to guide China's development which have undergone steady refinement. It is important to see them in totality so that we can find out the strengths and weaknesses of the various initiatives and their wider significance. If we take them in isolation we miss much of their meaning.

The ideas of Mao Zedong, Deng Xiaoping and their successors have contributed many insights to Marxist theoretical corpus as well as to theory and practice of social transformation. Contemporary social science rooted in the West is yet to place these ideas at the core of theoretical knowledge. Many Marxist scholars who have studied them are often centered on the question whether they remained Marxist or had turned revisionist and whether China already had become a capitalist country. We have addressed these issues in this volume with a view to finding out why did the Chinese communist leaders opted for the particular line of thought and action.

Understanding the considerations underlying policies is important to assess them. Contemporary China is a great success story in many respects. Today's China is not a socialist society, but the discourse on socialism continues in China. China's experiences with building socialism under Mao Zedong and during the reform period have posed many new questions for building 'socialism in the 21st century'. That socialism had to address class as well as gender, caste, race exploitation, that it had to build a relationship of harmony between humans and nature, that it had to take questions of culture more seriously than before so that all languages, cultures and religions are treated with equal status, that socialism has to be more democratic in day-to-day practice than capitalism, from grass-roots level to national and global level through institutions- are new questions which democrats, socialists and all humanists are seized with today. Modern China's strides for democratic and socialist transformation through its zig zag course present much learning for humanity.

BASIC DEVELOPMENT INFORMATION ON CHINA

(Tables I-IV which may be used for ready reference, are taken from Manoranjan Mohanty, *China's Success Trap: Lessons for Development Theory*, Founder's Day lecture delivered on 16 April 2013 at Madras Institute of Development Studies, Chennai.)

Table I. Human Development Indicators: China, India and US

	China	*India*	*United States*
Human Development Index (country rank)			
2006	81	126	8
2011	101	134	4
2012	101	136	3
Human Development Index: Trends	1975 : 0.527	0.413	0.868
	1980 : 0.407	0.345	0.843
	1990 : 0.495	0.410	0.878
	2000 : 0.590	0.463	0.907
	2005 : 0.637	0.507	0.923
	2010 : 0.689	0.547	0.934
	2011 : 0.695	0.551	0.936
	2012 : 0.699	0.554	0.937
Life Expectancy at Birth (years)	1970-75 : 63.2	50.7	71.5
	2005 : 71.9	62.9	77.4
	2010 : 73.5	64.4	79.6
	2012 : 73.7	65.8	78.7
Infant Mortality Rate/per thousand ('0000) live births	1970 : 85	1970 : 127	1970 : 20
	2000 : 32	2000 : 69	2000 : 7
	2005 : 23	2005 : 56	2005 : 6
	2010 : 16	2010 : 50	2010 : 7
Under Five Mortality Rate	1970 : 120	1970 : 202	1970 : 26
	2000 : 40	2000 : 96	2000 : 8
	2005 : 27	2005 : 74	2005 : 7
	2010 : 18	2010 : 63	2010 : 8
GDP (Billion US$)	2004 : 1,931.7	691.2	11,711.8
(2005 US$ PPP)	2011: 9,970.6	3,976.5	13,238.3
GDP Per Capita (PPP in US$)			
2005	6,757	3,452	41,810
2009	6,828	3,296	45,989
2011 (2005 PPP$)	7,418	3,203	42.486

Annual Growth Rate (GDP %)	1975-2005 : 8.4	3.4	2.0
	1990-2005: 8.8	4.2	2.5
	2008-2012: 9.3	6.9	1.7
Human Poverty Index Rank (2006)	26	55	16
Population below Income Poverty Line (%)			
1900-2003 (PPP US$1)	16.6	34.7	–
2000-2009 (PPP US$1.25)	15.9	41.6	–
2002-2011 (PPP US$1.25)	13.1	32.7	–
National Poverty Line (%)			
1990-2003 (PPP US$1)	4.6	28.6	–
2000-2009 (PPP US$1.25)	2.8	27.5	–
2002-2012 (PPP US$1.25)	2.8	29.8	–
Population with sustainable access to improved sanitation (%)	1990 : 23	14	–
	2004 : 44	33	–
	2008 : 45	69	–
Population undernourished (%)	1990-92: 16	25	2.5
	2001-03: 12	20	2.5
	2004-06: 10	22	<5

Source: Human Development Report, 2006 (New York: Palgrave Macmillan, 2006), 2007-08, 2010, 2011, 2013 (New Delhi: Academic Foundation, 2013) IMF: *World Economic Outlook Data Base*, April, 2011, 2012, (Accessed Online on 15 May and 23 September 2012), October 2012.
World Bank: *World Development Indicators*, 2012.

Table II. Inequality in China, India and US

	Survey Year	*Share of Income or Expenditure Poorest 10%*	*Share of Income or Expenditure Poorest 20%*	*Share of Income or Expenditure Richest 20%*	*Share of Income or Expenditure Richest 10%*	*Gini Co-efficient*
China	2001	1.8	4.7	50	33.1	44.7
	2005	1.8	5.0	47.9	32.0	42.5
India	1999-2000	3.9	8.9	43.3	28.5	32.5
	2005	3.8	8.6	42.4	28.3	33.4
US	2000	1.9	5.4	45.8	29.9	40.8
						40.8 (2000-10)

Source: UNDP: *Human Development Report*, 2006, 2010, 2011.
World Bank: *World Development Indicators*, 2012.

Table III. Energy and Environment

	China	*India*	*US*
GDP per unit of energy use (2000 PPP US$ per kg of oil equivalent)	1980 : 1.3 2003 : 4.5	3.3 5.3	2.8 4.5
Carbon dioxide emission (Per capita tons)	1980 : 1.5 2003 : 3.2 2008: 5.3 2009: 5.83	0.5 1.2 1.5 1.38	20.1 19.8 18.0 17.67
Share of world total of carbon dioxide emissions 2003	16.5	5.1	23.0
Greenhouse gas emissions per capita (tons of carbon dioxide equivalent)	2005: 1.5 2010: 1.38*	0.7 1.38	3.7 18
Total Greenhouse Gas emissions (million tons)	2008 : 6803 2009 : 7710.50	1473.73 1602.12	5833.13 5424.53

Source: UNDP, *Human Development Report*, 2006, 2010, 2011, 2013.
**Source: The Guardian* (31 January 2011)

Table IV. China's Vital Statistics 2008-12

Categories	*2008*	*2009*	*2010*	*2011*	*2012*
GDP (100 million yuan)	314045	340903	401513	473104	519322
Growth rates (%)	9.6	9.2	10.4	9.3	7.8
Newly increased employed in Urban areas (10,000 persons)	1113	1102	1168	1221	1226
Year –end Foreign Exchange Reserves (100 million USD)	19460	23992	28473	31811	33116
Growth rate (%)	27.3	23.3	18.7	11.7	4.1
Agriculture (Out-put of grains -10,000 tons)	52871	53082	54648	57121	58957
Growth rates (%)	5.4	0.4	2.9	4.5	3.2
Industrial Value Added (100 million yuan)	130260	135240	160722	188470	199860
Growth rates (%)	9.9	8.7	12.1	10.4	7.9
Imports (100 million USD)	11326	10059	13962	17435	18178
Exports (100 million USD)	14307	12016	15778	18984	20489
New Entrants into Education (10,000)					
General tertiary education	608	640	662	682	689
Secondary vocational education	812	869	870	814	761

Senior secondary education	837	830	836	851	845
R&D Investment (100 million yuan)	4616	5802	7063	8687	10240
Amount of Health Workers (10,000 persons)	517	554	588	620	650
Per-capita Disposable Income					
Rural (yuan)	4761	5153	5919	6977	7917
(%)	(8.0)	(8.5)	(10.9)	(11.4)	(10.7)
Urban (yuan)	15781	17175	19109	21810	24565
(%)	(8.4)	(9.8)	(7.8)	(8.4)	(9.6)
Number of Phone Subscribers (10,000 persons)					
Year-end no. of fixed phone subscribers	34036	31373	29434	28512	27815
Year-end no. of mobile phone subscribers	64125	74721	85900	98625	111216

Source: *Statistical Communiqué of the People's Republic of China on the 2012 National Economic and Social Development.*
(http://www.stats.gov.cn/english/newsandcomingevents/t20130222_40284607.htm

CPC CONGRESS AND MEMBERSHIP SINCE 1945

Party Congress	*Year*	*Party Leader*	*Total Membership*
7th	1945*	Mao Zedong	1,211,128
8th	1956	Mao Zedong	10,734,384
9th	1969	Mao Zedong	20,000,000
10th	1973	Mao Zedong	28,000,000
11th	1977	Hua Guofeng	35, 000,000
12th	1982	Hu Yaobang	39,650,000
13th	1987	Zhao Ziyang	46,000,000
14th	1992	Jiang Zemin	51,000,000
15th	1997	Jiang Zemin	58,000,000
16th	2002	Hu Jintao	66,000,000
17th	2007	Hu Jintao	73,000,000
18th	2012	Xi Jinping	82,000,000

**Note:* From 1945 till 1976 Mao Zedong was the Chairperson of the CPC. At the 11th Congress in 1977 Hua Guofeng was elected as the Chairperson. The office of the Chairperson was replaced by that of General Secretary at the 12th Congress in 1982.
Source: *People's Daily Online*. http://english.cpc.people.com.cn/ http://english.people.com.cn/90785/7910578.html

1

Maoism: A Twenty-first Century Profile

Maoism or Mao Zedong Thought?

The use of the term "Maoism" (*maozhuyi* in Chinese) in official documents of the Communist Party of China (CPC) was not allowed by Mao Zedong (1893-1976) during his lifetime. He decreed that the exalted term, *ism* should be reserved for the founders of communism and communist movement, namely Marx and Lenin. Mao considered his own ideas as less fundamental than those of Marx and Lenin pointing out that the CPC leadership with him as chairperson had mainly applied the basic theories of Marx and Lenin creatively, to the concrete conditions of the Chinese revolution. Deferring to his wishes the CPC theoreticians used the term, Thought (*sixiang*) which was first used in the seventh congress of the CPC in 1945 and then more systematically from 1965 onwards. During the Cultural Revolution (1966-1976) the CPC ideology was described as Marxism-Leninism-Mao Zedong Thought. It is interesting that in post-Mao China when Deng Xiaoping's ideas on 'reforms and open door' crystallized into a line, the CPC's 14th Congress in October 1992 called it 'Deng Xiaoping *Theory* (*lilun*) of Building Socialism with Chinese Characteristics'. Thereafter, Jiang Zemin's *important thoughts (zhongyao sixiang)* on Three Represents announced in the sixteenth party congress in 2002 and Hu Jintao's *Scientific Outlook (kexue guan)* on development put into the CPC constitution in 2007 carefully avoided assuming the theoretical levels of either Mao or Deng.

That however, has not prevented the widespread use of the term Maoism all over the world signifying the existence of a set of ideological principles, especially on people's democratic revolution and socialism. Whereas debates on the choice of revolutionary strategy brought to the focus Mao's theory derived from the Chinese revolution, Mao's ideas on what was the correct path to socialism became central reference points for scrutinizing the policy changes in the Soviet Union and reasons for its collapse as also assessing the reforms policies initiated by Deng.

When communist parties in different countries split, first over their stand on the ideological debates between the Communist Party of the Soviet Union (CPSU) and the CPC during 1959-1964 the then radical wings had added in parenthesis Marxist. Subsequently, when further splits took place in the wake of the Chinese Cultural Revolution and the issue of armed struggle or parliamentary path to socialism, many parties split further and the radical wings called themselves 'Marxist-Leninist'. When further splits took place among them, the most radical communist formations among them called themselves Maoist. There are two communist parties in South Asia with large-scale mass base which carry this name. One is the Communist Party of India (Maoist) formed after the merger of CPI-ML (People's War) and Maoist Communist Centre in 2004 which has an extensive support base in the tribal areas of central India. Another is the Communist Party of Nepal (Maoist) renamed Unified Communist Party of Nepal (Maoist) which was engaged in agrarian armed struggle from 1996 till 2006 when it participated in a popular uprising against the monarchy in Nepal and joined the electoral process to win the largest number of seats in the Constituent Assembly and in 2011 led a coalition government in Nepal for the second time. Its political programme presents the Maoist party as an organization committed to a creative Marxist-Leninist-Maoist programme called 'socialism in the 21st century'. Besides these two mass parties there are numerous Maoist parties and groups in different parts of the world.

Yet, Maoism like Marxism and Leninism was one of the

most debated subjects of the 20th century and is most likely to remain so in the 21st century in the face of the expanding process of capitalist globalization. This is because the formulations advanced by Mao and the later Maoists, challenge some of the dominant assumptions relating to the basic issues of struggle for liberation, equality, justice and self-development in course of social transformation in all societies.

Maoism in Post-Mao China

In China itself assessment of Maoism has varied between official verdict, elite opinions and popular adoration, especially in the countryside. In the immediate aftermath of the death of Mao and fall of the Gang of Four in 1976 a powerful current had emerged which was characterized as 'de-Maoization'. But Deng Xiaoping took the lead to reorient that trend and in a CPC Central Committee Plenum in 1981, a Resolution on Certain Questions in Party History for the post-1949 period was passed which set the official framework on treating Mao's role in contemporary China. The Deng leadership followed Mao's own method of discriminating evaluation of Stalin after Khrushchev's de-Stalinization in 1956. According to Mao he was 70 per cent right – for eliminating feudalism, building a strong industrial country and defending the Soviet Union in the face of Nazi and Fascist attacks during World War II. But he was 30 per cent wrong for abandoning democratic centralism and following absolute centralism and liquidating his opposition. Similarly, without mentioning the proportion, the CPC resolution recorded Mao's contribution in formulating the line and strategy for China's new democratic revolution that created massive popular support for the CPC among the peasantry, defeated the Japanese during the war of 1937-1945 and Guomindang during the civil war of 1946-1949 and founded the People's Republic of China. At the same time, the Resolution squarely criticized the economic ideas and policies of Mao Zedong during the 1958-1976 period starting from the Great Leap Forward till the end of the Cultural Revolution. Repudiation of the Cultural Revolution theory of class struggle paved the way for the reforms and open door line of Deng

Xiaoping proclaimed by the Third Plenum of the Eleventh Central Committee in December 1978.

There were signs of greater acknowledgment of Mao's contribution beginning with the celebration in 2009 of the sixtieth anniversary of the founding of the PRC. Many scholars and Party leaders took a holistic view of China's achievements rather than attributing the great economic successes of China only to the thirty years of reforms. As recognized abroad, now it was admitted in Chinese official circles that rural transformation through land reforms, cooperatives and finally collectives during the years of the People's Communes, the effort to universalize literacy and primary health care and bringing women to agricultural work besides building rural infrastructure during the Mao period had created a foundation for the success of the later reforms under Deng and his successors. In his speech on the occasion of the ninetieth anniversary of the founding of the CPC on July 1, 2011, CPC General Secretary acknowledged the 'great theoretical achievement' of Mao Zedong Thought which " resolved in a systematic way the issue of how to accomplish the new democratic revolution and socialist revolution in China, a big semi-colonial and semi-feudal country in the East and made painstaking efforts to explore the issue of what kind of socialism China should build and how to build it, thereby making new and creative contributions to enriching Marxism." (*News from China*, vol. XXIII, no. 7, July 2011, p. 7)

While the CPC discourse on Mao focuses on the theory of the new democratic revolution and critique of the cultural revolution, the Maoist understanding of the contemporary world has remained an important element of the Maoist discourse the world over. Underlying all three elements are some of the philosophical formulations on dialectics, especially on contradictions and practice which have been the basic premises of forming the Maoist outlook.

Mao and the Chinese Revolution

Mao Zedong was elected as the Chairperson of the CPC at the Zunyi conference of the Party in January 1935 in the middle of the Long March. He held that position in the Party till his death in September 1976. Born in a peasant family in Hunan, Mao was greatly influenced by the New Culture Movement and its organ, *New Youth* (*Xin Qingnian*). Joining as an Assistant Librarian in Peking University he came into contact with Li Lisan and Chen Duxiu, leading intellectuals of the time and was inspired by the Russian Revolution. The May Fourth Movement of 1919 produced new forces of nationalism and social transformation of which Mao Zedong was an integral part. He attended the founding conference of the CPC in Shanghai on July 1, 1921 and thereafter worked among the peasants of Hunan on agrarian issues. In 1927 Mao wrote his Report on an Investigation of the Peasant Movement in Hunan that recorded instances of peasant resistance to landlords and has remained a landmark formulation on the revolutionary potentiality of the peasants in the Marxist tradition which had underrated the role of the peasants thus far. After the first United Front of KMT and CPC (1924-1927) collapsed and the KMT regime of Chiang Kai-shek launched a countrywide onslaught on the communists, Mao Zedong went to the countryside to organize armed resistance of the peasants in the Hunan-Jiangxi border region. During the period of 1927-31 he set up base areas and organized them into Soviets in the region. In 1931 Mao was elected as the Chairperson of the Central Soviet Government in Jiangxi.

The Jiangxi Soviet period was known for radical agrarian policies with communists carrying out campaigns to take over landlords' land and distributing them among the landless. That was also the period which saw debates over strategy of the Chinese revolution with the dominant party leadership of Li Lisan, supported by the Communist International with headquarters in Moscow favouring urban workers' uprisings as the main line while Mao and his group arguing for agrarian revolution. In the meantime the KMT government of Chiang Kai-shek intensified its military campaigns against the communists and succeeded in forcing the Jiangxi Soviet government to evacuate. Hence in October 1934 Mao and the Red Army left their headquarters in Ruijin and began the famed

8000-mile Long March in the direction of the north. The Japanese, in the meanwhile, had occupied Machuria and set up a puppet government called Manchukuo and were slowly extending their control. The call of the CPC and the Red Army during the Long March was to build a united national defence against the Japanese imperialists. The Long March cost the Red Army many lives due to hardships en route and also frequent armed attacks by the KMT. But by the end of the Long March in Baoan in Shaanxi Province in October 1935 and by the time of setting up the base area in Yanan in 1937, the national opinion in favour of the CPC line had grown tremendously. The second United Front of the CPC with the KMT (1937-1945) was designed differently so as not to give up the base areas to the KMT or merge the Red Army units with the KMT's. They fought the Japanese army in different areas with their own armies. In course of this anti-Japanese war, Mao devised many new strategies and tactics of the people's war. After the defeat of Japan in 1945 there were talks for a coalition government between KMT and CPC which broke down resulting in the civil war. By the end of the anti-Japanese war the CPC's popular support had surged as had its armed strength. They liberated area after area from KMT control in the north, moved to Beijing in January 1949 and crossed Yangze river and secured Shanghai in April. On October 1, 1949 Mao Zedong proclaimed the founding of the People's Republic of China announcing the victory of the CPC-led new democratic revolution with his famous statement, "Chinese people have stood up".

It is in course of the trials and errors of the Chinese communist movement that the CPC under Mao evolved its revolutionary strategy. The most important formulations were articulated by Mao Zedong during the Yanan period between 1937-1945. After the birth of the People's Republic, the experiences with building people's democracy or what Mao called New Democracy and attempts to bring about a transition to socialism raised many debates with Mao at the centre. Those debates surrounding Mao's policies during the Great Leap Forward (1958) and the Cultural Revolution (1966-1976) brought out Mao's theoretical perspective on socialism. Many of these debates were conducted globally in response to the developments in the Soviet Union in addition to being critical reflections on China's own development experiences.

New Democratic Revolution

The 'three magic weapons' of the Chinese revolution according to Mao Zedong were the united front, the communist party and the people's army. They summed up the theory and strategy of the communist movement as it crystallized in course of the anti-Japanese war and the civil war. The special feature of the united front was the mobilization of the peasantry in alliance with the workers and the inclusion of the national bourgeoisie in it. On both these issues there were many controversies in the international communist movement as well as among the various factions in the CPC. Mao had already underlined the significance of the peasant upsurge in Hunan and now based in the countryside the main political support came from the peasants. The CPC factions of Li Lisan and Wang Ming which pushed for proletarian uprisings in the cities were eventually sidelined by Mao who had now gained influence as the head of the Jiangxi Soviet. Similarly, the debate on the national bourgeoisie took a new turn. In 1920 Lenin had favoured the inclusion of the national bourgeoisie in the united front in opposition to views of M.N. Roy. After the collapse of the KMT-CPC united front in 1927 it was difficult to pursue this line. But in view of the grave danger arising out of the unfolding aggression by Japanese forces, the CPC under Mao's leadership differentiated between comprador bourgeoisie that was pro-imperialist and national bourgeoisie that was anti-imperialist and choosing to align with the latter.

The communist party too had some special characteristics in the Chinese situation. It had started as a vanguard organization of the workers. But in the 1930s its peasant base expanded very fast. In course of the Long March its platform was one of national liberation from Japanese imperialism. While the KMT as the major national political force at the time pursued a strategy to first fight the 'communist bandits' and then face the Japanese, the CPC was regarded as a force of Chinese nationalism that had an agrarian base. During the Yanan period the CPC underwent much ideological churning to inculcate its specific understanding of Marxism and Leninism. Mao stressed the need to practise 'mass line' or learning from the masses and leading the masses which was the method of party-building during the Yanan period. This doctrine was later upheld as the CPC's way of practising democratic centralism as an alternative to Stalin's method of authoritarian centralism. Ideological education was yet another feature of Yanan communism.

'Without a people's army, the people have nothing' is a famous statement of Mao after the massacre of the communists by the KMT army in 1927. The organization of the Workers and Peasants Red Army in 1927 under the leadership of the CPC was the beginning of agrarian armed struggle as the principal form of the new democratic revolution. Its strength dwindled significantly by the end of the Long March due to the KMT attacks and the hardships faced en route. When the second United Front was launched after the Xian Incident when Chiang Kai-shek was forced by his generals to agree to a united front with the CPC, the Red Army did not merge with the KMT Army. It only renamed its two segments, the New Fourth Army in the north and the Eighth Route Army in the South. At the start of the civil war with the KMT in 1946 by which time the strength of the CPC's armed forces had expanded vastly, it was reconstituted as the People's Liberation Army – which liberated China in 1949 and continues to be the arm of the Chinese state even today. The strategy and tactics of people's war that the CPC under Mao evolved during the anti-Japanese war became the principal feature of the Chinese revolution which has strategic significance for later revolutionary movements all over the world.

The strategy of people's war was devised in a situation where the enemy forces were strong in weapons and professional forces and were entrenched in cities. The revolutionary forces on the other hand had a great asset in having massive popular support. Turning people's support into a strategic advantage was the main characteristic of people's war. This was done by evolving forms of guerrilla warfare to entice the enemy and cripple, defeat and sometimes annihilate them. This warfare relied on intelligence gathering by people of the battle zones. The other major characteristic of the people's war was to liberate areas and create revolutionary bases with the objective of encircling the cities from the countryside and thus liberating the whole country. The bases were to some extent, embryonic zones of the future new democratic and socialist society. The CPC carried out moderate land reforms with rent reduction campaigns, set up united front committees of government, launched production drives, provided relief to the poor. All these measures only added to the legitimacy of the CPC among the peasant masses. Thus the strategy of the people's war was the main form of the agrarian revolution.

Why was it called a new democratic revolution? After a series of writings such as Problems of Strategy in China's Revolutionary War (1936) On Protracted War (1938), Chinese Revolution and the Chinese Communist Party (1939), Mao wrote his major essay On New Democracy in January 1940 where he spelt out the theory and strategy of the new democratic revolution. In the Marxist-Leninist tradition so far the old democratic revolution, such as the French Revolution was led by the bourgeoisie. In Russia, the bourgeois democratic revolution had in many ways grown into a socialist revolution by the workers' uprising leading to the Bolshevik Revolution in 1917. The specific conditions obtaining in China had two distinct features according to Mao. One was the semi-colonial situation in China which had made China a country of colonial enclaves and multiple interests of colonial powers since the Opium War of 1840. At the same time, China was a semi-feudal society with the landed gentry dominating the social system where the development of the class of the bourgeoisie was limited. Thus the new democratic revolution was an anti-colonial and anti-feudal revolution. The principal contradiction was between imperialism, feudalism on the one hand and the people on the other. This is why it is also called the people's democratic revolution with the goal of setting up a people's democracy, not a bourgeois democracy. That section of the bourgeoisie which played the role of the agent of imperialism was called the comprador bourgeoisie which was part of the enemy forces. The united front of people fighting the enemy forces consisted of the four classes, namely, workers, peasants, petty bourgeoisie and the national bourgeoisie. Mao formulated an interesting characterization describing the four class united front as one with working class as the leader and peasants as the main force thus putting it in the Leninist tradition of having the communist party as the vanguard of the proletariat. That explained why the communist party had to lead a new democratic revolution. The mass of intellectuals, writers and middle class activists who joined the Anti-Japanese University in Yanan and other campaigns were an important part of the united front. Having a major section of the business class who were anti-Japanese and anti-KMT contributed to the effective mobilization strategy of the CPC.

The significance of the new democratic revolution was such that despite the criticisms relating to Mao's policies during the Great Leap and the Cultural Revolution, the official evaluation of Mao Zedong in China has remained highly positive. Its theoretical and strategic significance has been vindicated by the fact that many communist movements in former colonies in Asia, Africa and Latin America accepted the new democratic revolution as their political line. The CPC described this perspective as the creative application of Marxism-Leninism to the concrete conditions of the Chinese situation. As such it also opened up possibilities of creative application of revolutionary legacies of the Bolshevik as well as Chinese revolutions to concrete conditions of revolutions in various countries. The two unique aspects of the new democratic revolution were the mobilization of the peasantry and the broad united front mobilization on the platform of nationalism which included the national bourgeoisie. Both these dimensions had critical relevance to the populous agrarian societies in the third world which suffered in the hands of colonialism or in the recent decades also neo-colonialism.

Yet, critics of Mao pointed out the fact that Mao undermined working class leadership and promoted 'agrarian socialism' and 'peasant nationalism' deviating from classical Marxist-Leninist premises. Others criticize Mao for aligning with patriotic entrepreneurs temporarily in the early years of 'New Democracy' and attacking them soon after by initiating nationalization policies. The reform and open door policies initiated by Deng, re-emphasized the role of the entrepreneur class as a part of the 'people's democratic dictatorship' and established links between Mao's 'new democratic revolution' and the 'preliminary stage of socialism' in which the 'socialist market economy' developed and achieved spectacular economic growth in China.

Mao's Perspective on Socialism and the Cultural Revolution

Mao's ideas on building socialism which led him to launch the Great Leap Forward in 1958 and the Cultural Revolution in 1966 have been subjected to much criticism in China during the reform period and also by development analysts in the liberal and neo-liberal mould all over the world. These mass campaigns caused enormous hardships to millions of people. Yet it is important to understand the Maoist perspective which guided those initiatives. Essentially these campaigns, especially the Cultural Revolution raised qualitative questions about the nature of socialism affirming that socialism was not only about achieving high growth of production as in the case of capitalist systems, but it was to be based on the socialist vision of creating an egalitarian society with socialist values and moving towards a classless society. This view was articulated by Mao in the course of debates with the CPSU under Khrushchev and similar debates within the CPC first during 1956-1958 and then during 1965-1967. This perspective was formulated by the Maoist leadership in 1967 as 'the theory of continuing class struggle in socialist society' also known as the theory of continuous revolution which was the perspective underlying the Cultural Revolution.

The theory of continuous revolution had three premises: First, even after the bourgeoisie is overthrown from political power and even from economic power, it continues its dominance in the cultural realm. Second, there are dangers of restoration of the power of the bourgeoisie in socialist society which still contains many surviving elements of bourgeois economy, in addition to the cultural realm. Mao pointed out that there was a restoration of capitalism in the Soviet Union due to the revisionist policies of Khrushchev. Third, therefore, the proletariat must continue the revolutionary class struggle until the onset of the communist stage. This was the basis of initiating mass campaigns against 'capitalist roaders' who included Liu Shaoqi, President of the PRC and Deng Xiaoping and their supporters all over China during the Cultural Revolution. Ideological campaigns through mass meetings and rallies spread throughout China. Schools and colleges were closed asking students and intellectuals to perform labour with peasants in the countryside and acquire proletarian culture. The Little Red Book with quotations from Mao Zedong became the reference for guiding action. Red Guards and revolutionary committees were a ubiquitous phenomenon replacing all political institutions. A cult of Mao was created. The pro-Mao faction of the PLA led by Lin Biao established its control. When Mao tried to curb Lin Biao's power then there was a failed coup by Lin who died in an air crash while fleeing in October 1971. Thereafter a new group, a Gang of Four with Mao's wife Jiang Qing tried to establish its control to carry on its line of the Cultural Revolution. After the death of Mao in September 1976 the Gang of Four was arrested by Hua Guofeng who had been designated by Mao to succeed him. In the next two years debates within the Party went on regarding the validity of the Cultural Revolution line and politics. In December 1978, Deng Xiaoping led the Central Committee to completely repudiate the Cultural Revolution and announce the 'shift of focus from class struggle to economic construction'. Thus the new line of 'Reform and Open Door' was launched by the Deng leadership which has transformed China into the second largest economy of the world in 2010 with vast improvement in people's living standards.

The Deng leadership had four major criticisms against Mao's theory and the Cultural Revolution. Firstly, socialism was not about poverty, but improving material conditions of people to achieve an egalitarian society. Indeed, the growth rate under the reforms has grown with modern infrastructure and better living conditions for all and substantial reduction in poverty. Second, mass campaigns in the name of fighting class enemies suspended all institutions, led to arbitrary use of power and harassed and killed many innocent people . Indeed, since 1978 the organs of state and the Party have met regularly according to the constitution and even ensured smooth transition of leadership from one generation to another. Third, the theoretical premise that treats culture or ideology as autonomous is, according to the critics, an idealist deviation of Mao which put superstructure independent of the economic base, thus violating the tenets of dialectical and historical materialism. It is this perspective which invoked workers to work not on material incentives but ideological incentives during the Mao era. That perspective put so much emphasis on self-reliance as a principle that during the Great Leap Forward there was severe scarcity of food and caused a massive famine in which millions of people perished. The Deng regime stressed the need for 'open door' within the country and worldwide to share the knowledge and resources of others. Fourthly, the egalitarianism promoted during the Cultural Revolution was an attempt to artificially create conditions of equality irrespective of the contribution made by a worker. The many Maoist policies including the people's communes were regarded as 'eating from the iron bowl' or everyone getting the same out of a common fund. The rural communes were dismantled and a Household Contract Responsibility system was introduced in the early years of the reforms which distributed land equitably in proportion to the number of the members in the family on long-term contract for farming by the household.

Yet the debates on the questions raised by Mao on building of socialism are not closed. As the Chinese leadership grapples with the consequences of the reforms and the world debates the social and environmental consequences of neo-liberal globalization, the qualitative questions about the nature of socialism in particular and development in general, will continue to be raised.

Culture, Ethnicity and Maoism

The ideological focus of the Cultural Revolution on classes and class struggle has clouded a closer discussion on the treatment of ethnicity in the Maoist theoretical framework. But taking Mao's life and works as a whole, it is possible to discern two aspects of his approach to the ethnic question. One being the necessity to protect cultural identity of every group in the process of revolutionary transformation and the other being the need to curb chauvinism either of the small group or the large group. But before that a clarification may be in order. Until the reforms period, this issue was discussed under the category of the 'nationality question'. But as China's social science discourse got increasingly reshaped by the Western vocabulary, the same Chinese word 'minzu' was now translated mostly as an 'ethnic group'. In the Marxist discourse, a social group with shared cultural identity seeking political safeguards for its identity was always referred to in the writings and policies of Lenin and Stalin and subsequently of Mao as nationality. The preference for the term 'ethnic identity' during the reform period in China during the 1980s coincided with the growing Western emphasis on the significance of non-class social formations as against the primacy of class. In the aftermath of the Cultural Revolution as the attempts were made to de-emphasize class struggle the shift from nationality discourse to ethnic identity was not surprising. But the significance of the cultural identity of a group and evolving a viable policy has remained a challenge throughout the history of the PRC.

The two elements of the Maoist approach to the ethnic question were stated eloquently by Mao in his speech at the enlarged meeting of the CPC Politbureau on April 25, 1956, entitled, *On Ten Major Relationships*: "We put the emphasis on opposing Han chauvinism. Local nationality chauvinism must be opposed too, but generally that is not where our emphasis lies....The minority nationalities have all contributed to the making of China's history." Discussing the relationship between the Hans and the minority nationalities he mentioned how "all through the ages, the reactionary rulers, chiefly from Han nationality, sowed feelings of estrangement among our various nationalities and bullied the minority peoples." In this speech as far back as in 1956, Mao had described the treatment of the minority nationalities in the Soviet Union as ''abnormal'' and called upon the CPC to learn lessons from it. Indeed, this was one of the contradictions which got accentuated in the succeeding years leading to the collapse of the USSR in 1991.

Mao reiterated the same perspective in another important essay the following year. In a speech to the Supreme State Conference on February 27, 1957 entitled, "On the Correct Handling of Contradictions among People", Mao characterized both Han chauvinism and local nationality chauvinism as harmful to the unity of nationalities and described their relationship as a "contradiction among people", therefore a non-antagonistic contradiction to be resolved in a framework of ''unity-criticism-unity". This was different from the antagonistic contradiction between people and the enemy or between the classes who constitute the united front on the one hand and the oppressor classes on the other. The former contradiction is to be handled through peaceful negotiations while the latter involved coercion and suppression. Mao explained that minority nationalities constituted six per cent of the population but occupied over fifty per cent of China's territory possessing massive natural resources. But respecting what Mao called "the human factor" was essential for using those resources for building socialism. It should be noted that the minority population had gone up to over eight per cent by 2010.

How was the nationality question or the "human factor" handled by the Chinese regime under Mao and by his successors? The record is not very encouraging. Even though the Maoist approach of the 1956-57 broadly continues to remain the official perspective of the CPC its performance on the ground has failed to eliminate discontent in the minority areas. Even before coming to power, the CPC under Mao's leadership had pursued the policy of forging solidarity between the Hans and the minority nationalities. The Jiangxi Soviet Constitution of 1931 had a provision for the right to self-determination of nationalities including the right to secession. In the course of the Long March the Red Army travelled through the minority nationality areas and secured much support among them in the north-western region. The PRC Constitution of 1954 affirmed by its later versions regards the PRC as a multi-national state. Article 4 of the PRC Constitution declares all nationalities of China as equal, protects the rights of minority nationalities and prohibits discrimination against and oppression of them. The six big minority areas (inner Mongolia, Heilongjiang, Guangxi, Tibet, Ningxia and Xinjiang) were constituted as Autonomous Regions with their own constitutions and autonomous organs of power. There are 55 minority nationalities whose language and culture are recognized and protected by law.

Yet the CPC policy has failed to respond to the democratic aspirations of minority groups of Xinjiang and Tibet. Two strands of thought which evolved as major currents in the modern history of China also have origins in Maoist practice, have contributed to this situation. Firstly, the stress on nationalism and building a united China was a great commitment of the CPC during the anti-Japanese war, further reinforced during the cold war which kept Taiwan as a separate entity. Therefore the Chinese regimes treated territorial sovereignty as a firm value ruthlessly suppressing any challenge posed by minority groups. Secondly, during the Cultural Revolution when Mao was at the helm of affairs, the CPC faction in power promoted the idea that socialism would create conditions of equality irrespective of race, gender and ethnic identity. Religion was considered as an obstacle to that process. Religious practices were suppressed and religious places including mosques in Xinjiang and Buddhist monasteries in Tibet, in addition to Confucian temples in many parts of China were vandalized. Even though Mao Zedong was referred to as the "great leader of all the nationalities of China" the Cultural Revolution greatly alienated China's minority nationalities from the CPC.

During the reforms period Deng Xiaoping and his successors took a number of major steps to recover ground and win over minorities. Religious places were rebuilt, religious practices were revived. Language, literature and culture were given a substantial boost. Massive economic investments were made and the areas were opened to foreign tourism and trade. Under the Western Region Development Strategy launched in 2000 large-scale construction projects were launched and poverty alleviation programmes achieved major success. However, even the numerous economic and cultural initiatives did not adequately respond to the political urges of the minority nationalities. Political leadership, especially Party leadership in the regions still remained in the hands of the Hans. Rebellious campaigns and self-determination movements persist in Tibet and Xinjiang which are regarded as "separatist" and subjected to severe repression in contemporary China.

Paradoxically, Maoism which took culture and superstructure seriously in its treatment of dialectical and historical materialism did not ensure correct handling of this contradiction among people in China. It is noteworthy that the Unified Communist Party of Nepal (Maoist) took up the issue of protecting the cultural and political rights of Nepal's ethnic minorities in the making of the Nepalese constitution during 2008-2011. However, only the future would show how effectively the Maoists deal with the issue of intersectionality of class, race, nationality, caste and gender in practice.

Maoism in the Global Political Tradition

Maoism does not figure prominently either in the Western discourses on Marxism or the discourses on development and transformation in the West. Paradoxically, communist movements and discourses on social transformation in the Asian, African and Latin American countries derive many insights and inspiration from the Maoist tradition. That is because they find the ideological creativity in Mao Zedong's theory and political practice as attractive. In the two philosophical essays of Mao, *On Practice* and *On Contradiction*, both written in 1937, the essential point made by Mao is that theory has to be derived from practice. Hence the innovative idea of new democratic revolution and many new formulations on socialism, however controversial they may be. While the new democratic revolution focussed on unity of people for national liberation, the theory of socialism stressed equality. In both cases, social differentiation was made essentially on class lines. The concept of 'people' (*renmin*) in People's Liberation Army, people's democracy and People's Republic of China clearly meant, as Mao put it, ninety-five per cent of the population against the enemies. This concept of people, representing the broadest possible spectrum of a united front was the central theme for revolution as well as social transformation according to the Maoist framework. But in practice, it often pursued class politics in such a way that it did not adequately respect the relative autonomy of ethnic identity.

On the gender issue the famous statement 'Women hold up half the sky', is attributed to Mao. During the Yanan period many women were placed in high positions and a large number of women joined the PLA. The PLA soldiers were scrupulous in maintaining dignity and rights of women in the war zones. The reform of the family under the Marriage Law in 1950 was a radical measure giving choice and equal rights in many spheres to women and men. The people's communes released women from household work and gave them opportunities to do agricultural work in the fields earning work points along with men. However, they got less work points than men. Mao is credited for taking many steps towards the liberation of women. But the structural inequalities accruing from property rights, job opportunities and above all feudal cultural beliefs still remain. Women are yet to obtain high leadership positions to any significant measure in the Chinese state or Party. The reforms may have accentuated gender inequities as men move to specialized technical jobs in a situation of high growth. Thus the trend of gender equity visible during the Maoist era may not have been sustained in the reform era as the dialectical relationship between class and gender with autonomous importance given to gender remained unresolved in China.

NOTES

Dirlik, Arif, Paul Healy and Nick Knight, *Critical Perspectives on Mao Zedong's Thought* (Amherst, N.Y.: Humanity Books, second edition, 1997).

Fitzgerald, C.P., *Mao Tse-tung and China* (London: Hodder and Stoughton, 1976).
Mao Zedong, "On New Democracy" in *Selected Works* (Beijing: Foreign Languages Press, 1965) Vol. 2.
Mao Zedong, *Four Essays on Philosophy* (Beijing: Foreign Languages Press, 1968).
Meisner, Maurice, *Mao Zedong: A Political and Intellectual Portrait* (Cambridge: Polity, 2007).
Mohanty, Manoranjan, *The Political Philosophy of Mao Zedong* (New Delhi: Macmillan, 1977, 2nd ed., Delhi: Aakar Books, 2012).
Pence, Jonathan, *Mao Zedong: A Life* (London: Penguin, 2006).
Schram, Stuart (ed), *Mao Tse-tung Unrehearsed: Talks and Letters 1956-71* (London: Penguin, 1974).
Schram, Stuart, *The Political Thought of Mao Tse-tung* (New York: Praeger, Revised edition 1969).
Resolution on CPC History (1949-81) (Beijing: Foreign Languages Press, 1981).

2

Mao's Portrait of Stalin

'Joseph Vissarionovich Stalin, greatest genius of the present age, great teacher of the world Communist movement, comrade-in-arms of the immortal Lenin, has departed from the world .... After the death of Lenin, Comrade Stalin led the Soviet people in building into a magnificent socialist society the first socialist state in the world .... Comrade Stalin carried out a comprehensive and epoch-making development of Marxist-Leninist theory and advanced Marxism to a new stage of development. Comrade Stalin creatively developed Lenin's theory concerning the law of uneven development of capitalism and Lenin's theory that socialism can first be victorious in one country; Comrade Stalin creatively contributed [to] the theory of the general crisis of the capitalist system; he contributed [to] the theory concerning the building of Communism in the Soviet Union, he contributed [to] the theory of the basic economic laws of modern capitalism and of socialism; he contributed [to] the theory of the revolution in colonial and semi-colonial countries. Comrade Stalin also creatively developed Lenin's theory on the building of the Party....'

'Chinese Communists and the Chinese people will further intensify the study of Stalin's teachings, of Soviet science and techniques to build their country....'

That was how Mao mourned the death of Stalin in March 1953.[1] Was it just a generous condolence message and a matter of formal courtesy, or was it a well-thought-out and carefully worded tribute which also contained Mao's evaluation of Stalin?

Is there a significant discrepancy between Mao's public and private evaluation of Stalin? Has the evaluation undergone a change during the past two decades? Questions like these can now be discussed in a not-so-helpless manner, for quite a few writings and speeches of Mao during the past twenty-five years, throwing new light on his estimate of Stalin, have recently been made available to the public.[2]

On reading these materials one gets the clear impression that Mao's 1953 evaluation of Stalin has not basically changed. However, as the experiences in the international communist movement and also in China's internal politics have accumulated and led to additional theoretical conclusions, the Stalin phenomenon has come in for further analysis and deeper scrutiny. Both for evolving a mode of socialist revolutionary politics and for an all-round struggle against tendencies of capitalist restoration Stalin's negative and positive aspects have become crucial reference points.

Correct and Incorrect Sides

Mao and many other leaders of the Communist Party of China (CPC) have always maintained a distinction between the merits and mistakes of Stalin. This was stated in Chinese responses to Khrushchev's wholesale denunciation of Stalin in 1956. In 1963 when the Communist Party of the Soviet Union (CPSU) branded the CPC as the 'defenders of the personality cult and peddlers of Stalin's erroneous ideas' the CPC replied: 'In defending Stalin, the Chinese Communist Party defends his correct side ... we do not defend his mistakes.'[3] The same kind of distinction was made earlier by Mao. In a party meeting at Chengdu, Mao said on March 10, 1958: 'When Stalin was criticized in 1956, we were on the one hand happy, but on the other hand apprehensive. It was completely necessary to remove the lid, to break down blind faith, to release the pressure and to emancipate thought. But we did not agree with demolishing him at one blow. They do not hang up his picture, but we do.'[4]

The correct side of Stalin was elaborated succinctly in Mao's condolence article in 1953 cited above. It is the most handsome tribute paid by Mao to Stalin for his contribution to the building of the first socialist state. Next comes the acknowledgement of his leadership during the war against the Nazis. In dealing with Stalin's theoretical achievements Mao has only listed the areas where Stalin made contributions to the already existing theories of Lenin or his forerunners. This list also carefully avoids any reference to Stalin's works on dialectical materialism. Thus a careful reading of Mao's 1953 mourning piece suggests that while Mao had reservations about Stalin's theoretical claims and was aware of his mistakes, he was more than willing to acknowledge his positive contribution to the development of the Soviet state which had enormous international significance.'

Stalin and the Chinese Revolution

While the correct and the laudable side of Stalin was magnified by Soviet economic assistance to China in the early 1950s, the incorrect and the erroneous aspect of Stalin was tainted by the fact that Stalin's guidance to the Chinese communists at certain stages of their revolution proved to be wrong and costly. Stalin's misleading advice figures repeatedly in Mao's speeches. In one place he says: 'The Chinese revolution won victory by acting contrary to Stalin's wills. Referring to Stalin's frequent suggestions to go slow in the final civil war against Chiang Kai-shek he says: 'The fake foreign devil (in Lu Xun's *True Story of Ah Q*) did not allow people to make revolution". But our Seventh Congress [April 1945] advocated going all out to mobilize the masses and to build up all available revolutionary forces to establish a new China....When our revolution succeeded, Stalin said it was a fake.'[7] The Polemic article on Stalin in September 1963 talked about this without any hesitation: 'Long ago the Chinese Communists had first-hand experience of some of his mistakes.... In the late twenties, the thirties and the early and middle forties, the Chinese Marxist-Leninists represented by Comrades Mao Zedong and Liu Shaoqi resisted the influence of Stalin's mistakes.... [8] Dealing with this issue in a talk in 1964 Mao said: 'Stalin realized that he had made some mistakes on the China problem, and they were by no means small mistakes.... He opposed our revolution and our seizure of political power.'[9]

An appreciation of Stalin's role in China's people's democratic revolution requires an independent exercise and we still do not have enough details to pass any judgment. But the way Mao perceives Stalin's role in this has become clearer with the availability of more evidence. His political opponents in the twenties and thirties draw their strength from the backing of the Comintern and particularly from Stalin. At the final stage of the civil war it was Stalin again who probably wanted a compromise between the CPC and the Kuomintang. Milovan Djilas records Stalin on this: 'True, we, too, can make a mistake! Here, when the war with Japan ended, we invited the Chinese comrades to reach an agreement as to how a modus vivendi with Chiang Kai-shek might be found. They agreed with us in word, but in deed they did it their own way when they got home: they mustered their forces and struck. It has been shown that they were right, and not we.'[10]

This assessment may be compared with Mao's indirect reference to Stalin's role in the Chinese revolution in the condolence message: 'He contributed his lofty wisdom to the problems of the Chinese revolution. And it was by following the teachings of Lenin and Stalin, and with the support of the great Soviet state and all the revolutionary forces of other countries, that the CPC and the Chinese people won their historic victory a few years ago.'[11] Mao here appears to be closely guarded in his statement about Stalin's role. He became more explicit in identifying Stalin's errors only after Khrushchev 'removed the lid'.

This experience might have led to a wholesale agreement between Mao and Khrushchev on denouncing Stalin. But, for good reasons, that did not happen. Mao led the Chinese communists to see both sides of Stalin and to learn from his successes as well as failures.

A Theoretical Formulation of the Stalin Question

Learning from Stalin was to be undertaken from a dialectical materialist viewpoint, according to the Chinese communists. This could start from defining the problem not in terms of the individual leader or the 'cult of personality' as Khrushchev put it, but by analysing the forces that led to centralization of power in the CPSU, enforcement of political terror and deviations in economic development in the USSR. Underlining the need to understand 'the ideological, social and historical roots' of the errors, the Stalin question was framed theoretically thus by the polemical article: 'In his way of thinking Stalin departed from dialectical materialism and fell into metaphysics and subjectivism on certain questions and, consequently, he was sometimes divorced from reality and from the masses. In struggles inside as well as outside the Party, on certain occasions and on certain questions he confused two types of contradictions which are different in nature, contradictions between ourselves and the enemy and contradictions among the people, and also confused the different methods needed in handling them.... In the matter of Party and government organization, he did not fully apply proletarian democratic centralism, and to some extent, violated it ....'[12]

An attempt to go deep into the roots of the Stalin phenomenon was demonstrated in April 1956 when in the *People's Daily* editorial, 'On the Historical Experiences of the Dictatorship of the Proletariat', the Chinese communists reflected on their own experiences. In this essay and in a much longer subsequent article in December 1956 entitled 'More on the Historical Experiences....' they suggested their method of 'mass line' politics as a possible guarantee against the rise of political terror. Mao's 1957 essay, *On the Correct Handling of Contradictions among the People*, came as the most serious attempt to comprehend theoretically the problem of class contradictions in socialist society.

All the writings of Mao since 1957 attempt to link up Stalin's errors with Khrushchev's revisionism by saying that both were departures from dialectical materialism and both arose out of metaphysical premises. As said earlier, 'mass line' politics is China's alternative to the Stalinist mode of politics. Similarly, in the realm of political economy of socialist construction Stalin's lopsided strategy of economic development which emphasized heavy industry was countered by Mao's strategy of comprehensive development. The Great Leap Forward in 1958 symbolized this approach in an ambitious way. In the late 1950s and early 60s as the new policies were gradually put into practice in the Soviet Union, Mao wanted his alternative course of socialist construction not only to take care of Stalin's deviations but also to fight against Khrushchev's revisionism. This search for a new path of progress led Mao in the direction of the theory of 'continuing the revolution under the dictatorship of the proletariat' through a series of 'great proletarian cultural revolutions'. Continuous revolutionary class struggle against the bourgeoisie, Mao thought, would keep the 'mass line' politics in operation and avoid the deviations of Stalin as well as the revisionism of Khrushchev. Thus Stalin's ghost is haunting Mao's library at (Zhongnanhai) where he had entertained Khrushchev.

The post-Stalin writings of Mao showed an increasing sophistication in the discussion on Stalin. There were frequent analyses of Stalin's method as well as his theoretical approach. His *Economic Problems of Socialism in the USSR* had been subjected to detailed commentaries by Mao. While discussing at great length a book on the Soviet Union's political economy, Mao extensively analysed Stalin's economic policies. Interestingly enough, he did not seem to ascribe much theoretical calibre to Stalin's successors in the Kremlin. Even for scrutinizing post-Stalin Soviet policies he links them up with Stalin and more often contrasts with Lenin's ideas.

Metaphysics in Stalin's Methodology

Mao attributes most of Stalin's errors to his methodology. Men in leadership positions should comprehend Marxist theory and apply the method of dialectical materialism. Stalin, on the other hand, was very often subjective in his judgment and took decisions according to his personal preferences. His approach contained more metaphysics and less dialectics. By this Mao is perhaps alluding to Stalin's whimsical decisions which did not stand the test of Marxist dialectical reasoning. Mao says: 'Methodology is a struggle between dialectics and metaphysics. Stalin made mistakes in dialectics. Negation of negations. The October Revolution negated capitalism but it refused to admit that socialism may be negated too. We believe that the world is both stable and unstable. Even socialism may cease to exist one day.'[13] Mao fears that abandonment of dialectics may even negate socialist achievements. At another place Mao says: 'Lenin's dialectics, Stalin's metaphysics and present-day dialectics – all this is also a negation of negation.'[14]

Giving an example of Stalin's lack of dialectical method, Mao cites how Stalin divorced technology from politics and heavily stressed the former in economic development: 'If technology decides everything, what about politics? If cadres [in Stalin's time they were more "expert" than "red"] decide everything, what about the masses? Lenin said it well: 'The Soviet plus electrification equals communism. The Soviet is politics, and electrification technology. The combination of politics and technology creates communism. Politics and technology are the unity of opposites. Their wedding will produce a son.'[15]

One of the reasons for Stalin's poor score in dialectics was that he was 'less studious' in the eyes of Mao: 'He rejected German philosophy (Kant and Fuerbach) and because Germany was defeated, he also rejected German military science. Germany's classical philosophy is the progenitor of Marxism.'[16] Contrast this with Marx, Engels and Lenin who 'studied energetically current and historical things and urged the people to do the same'.

It is well known that Mao himself was a voracious reader of both traditional as well as modern writings. From time to time, he initiated mass campaigns in China for 'study'. In contrast to the years of the Great Proletarian Cultural Revolution when Marxism was thought to be capsulized in the *Red Book* of quotations from Mao's writings, in later years the study of Marxist classics has been emphasized. During the campaign against Lin Biao most of his mistakes were attributed to the outlook of 'apriori idealism' which is a form of metaphysics. Lin Biao was also accused of having grossly neglected 'theoretical study'. However, the question may be asked whether study alone can help one acquire the dialectical method. In his essays *On Practice* and *Where Do Correct Ideas Come From*? Mao Zedong stressed the point that knowledge is obtained through continuous practice. In this respect, however, Stalin cannot be underrated. He participated in the Russian revolutionary struggle right from the beginning. Thus practice alone does not seem to guarantee correct dialectical understanding either. It is the continuous process of reasoning through practice in the light of earlier experiences and knowledge which can help. This is how an individual's subjective view is replaced by an objective view and metaphysics by dialectics.

'Overlord Flavour' in Stalin's Work-style

Stalin's metaphysics was manifested in his style of work. Mao presents a glaring contrast between this mode of functioning on the one hand, and the 'mass line' work-style which the CPC evolved since the Yanan days on the other. Mao says: 'We follow Lenin in the mass line and class struggle. We want to eliminate the bourgeoisie thoroughly (including its ideology), but without confiscating the property and destroying the people [person] of the bourgeoisie. Stalin did not promote mass line. He played favouritism and was too excessive in the class struggle.'[17]

Stalin was acutely aware of his high position in the international communist movement and this contributed to excessive centralization of decision-making power in his hands. In his attitude towards other leaders of the Soviet Union and of communist parties abroad Stalin felt very superior. Here is Mao's comparison of Lenin with Stalin on this point : 'His [Lenin's] reasoning is vivid and lively and he bares his heart to the people in his sincerity, without any hedging. The same holds true even in his struggle against the enemy. Comrade Stalin had a slight overlord flavour. Educated in a missionary school, he was not so good in dialectics, nor materialism. He was divorced from reality and did not handle successfully the mutual relations. He was relatively rigid.'[18]

Mao describes Stalin's airs of superiority as 'one-sidedness' and, therefore, not dialectical. Revolutionary movement involves both the leadership and the masses, and their roles have to be analysed dialectically. Mao referred to this on one occasion: 'Your post may be high, but still it won't do when he made a mistake. Wasn't Stalin's post high enough? It won't do when he made a mistake. Some people put on the airs of a veteran by saying: when I was making revolution, you were still crawling under the table! If you employ that line, people won't like to hear it. '[19]

This description of Stalin's work-style seems to be a gross understatement of Stalin's dictatorial mode of political operation. The way he built up a secret network of control to guard against opposition to him within or outside the party and the manner in which he took decisions have been publicized during Khrushchev's campaign of de-Stalinization. Mao does not discuss those issues in detail in these pages. However, at one place he says: 'Stalin taught the wrong thing to many people. They became metaphysical and stagnant in thought and consequently they committed political blunders. Whoever is in dissent is condemned. The penalty for counter-revolution is execution.... But actually Stalin could not enforce severe penalties. He did not execute or imprison all renegades. He put to death more people in 1936 and 1937, but fewer in 1938 and still fewer in 1939. This shows that we cannot kill all dissenters.'[20]

Even then Mao does go to the root of Stalinist terror by linking this work-style with the dialectical method and contrasting it with the CPC's 'mass line'. Yet the question remains as to what socio-economic conditions led to the weakening of the structure of the CPSU and built up a 'cult of personality'? Perhaps this had something to do with the pattern of socialist construction in the USSR after the death of Lenin.

Development by 'Walking on One Leg'

The pattern of economic development in the USSR caused continuous uneasiness in Mao's mind. In this field of political economy Stalin's model and Mao's model have crystallized into two alternative paths of socio-economic change. Ever since the Great Leap Forward these differences have been widely noted and discussed outside China. The new materials confirm these differences and at the same time throw light on the theoretical basis of the two alternative courses. Moreover, how Stalin's one-sidedness is grouped together with Khrushchev's is another revealing dimension of these writings.[21]

Mao's most serious comments on Stalin's economic ideas are contained in his 'Speech on the Book Economic Problems of Socialism in the Soviet Union (November 1958)' and in his 'Reading Notes on the Soviet Union's Political Economy (1961-1962)'. Commenting on Stalin's strategy of economic development, Mao says: 'In industry he stressed heavy industry, but not light industry. This also was walking on one leg. Within the mutual relationships of heavy industry he did not bring out the major aspect of the contradictions. He stressed heavy industry, calling steel the foundation and machinery the heart. We propose grain as the foundation in the agricultural aspect and steel as the foundation in the industrial aspect.'[22] Referring to Stalin's neglect of agriculture, Mao cautions against imbalanced accumulation of capital: 'Everybody wants to accumulate more and carry on some industry [industrialization] and this is well-intentioned. Stalin followed this kind of policy. In the 30 years from the founding of the state until 1953, Stalin never solved this problem.' Mao notes here that Stalin's successors took some steps to improve agriculture but essentially the pattern continued.[23] Khrushchev too was 'lame in one leg'. Mao says: 'Soviet heavy industry is too big and too centralized, disregarding the local areas. It stresses administration and lacks mass line.'[24]

Perhaps this imbalance would have been reduced had there been a correct understanding of the 'harmony and contradiction between the superstructure and the base in socialist society' and the 'internal contradictions among people'. Lopsided industrial development accentuated the internal contradictions between the workers of the large industries and the peasants of the countryside. Their incomes and standards of living became vastly unequal.[25] This was because Stalin visualized a complete correspondence between the superstructure and the base; and thought that if the character of the base changed into the socialist form, then the superstructure would accordingly change in harmony with it. Mao discussed this issue in the context of the CPC Eighth Congress declaration of 1956 (which he disapproved) that the main contradiction was no longer the one between the bourgeoisie and the proletariat, but between the advanced social system and the backward productive forces. The 1956 line had thus suggested that the important task before the CPC was to improve the productive forces. Mao compared this with Stalin's viewpoint and said that Stalin's one-sided approach identified the main tasks only at the production level and ignored similar work at the level of superstructure.[26] According to Mao, the socialist system and the productive forces will never be in 'perfect conformity'; they will have some areas of harmony and some areas of conflict.

In the light of Mao's notion of the great Proletarian Cultural Revolution which is a 'revolution in superstructure' to fight against the bourgeoisie, the discussion becomes even more significant. Neglect of the superstructure in Stalin's time and afterwards has been, according to Mao, one of the reasons for revisionism in the CPSU. Mao says: 'Stalin only discussed production relationships but did not mention superstructure [in his book], nor the relationship between the superstructure and the economic foundation.'[27] Giving an example of an area where superstructure is stressed in China, Mao points out: 'In China the cadres take part in labour; the workers take part in management; the cadres are sent down for [ideological] tempering; the old regulations and systems are destroyed. All these belong to the superstructure, to the ideological. Stalin only discussed economics, but not politics. Though he urged selfless labour, they would not work even one extra hour, and could not forget the self. The effect of man and the effect of the labourer were not discussed.'[28]

Going deeper into the theoretical question of one-sided development, Mao raised questions about the nature of the stage of socialism and its differences with communism in Stalin's framework. To hold back the transition from collectivization to 'socialist ownership by the whole people' is to deny the growth of communist elements in the socialist stage itself. That would mean mechanical isolation of ('distinct separation') the two stages of revolution. According to Mao, in certain spheres of the Soviet economy Stalin polarized the two elements: 'In regard to the socialist system, two kinds of ownership exist simultaneously in the socialist stage. They are opposites, and also united. Collective ownership contains the nucleus of the socialist ownership by the people. Its basic essence is collective ownership, but it also contains the element of the communist ownership by all the people.... In the nations under the leadership of the communist party, it is proper to allow the elements of communism to grow. Stalin did not solve this problem. He polarized the collective ownership, the socialist ownership by all the people, and the communist ownership by all the people. This is wrong.[29] Mao suggests that 'Communist factors should be allowed to grow in socialist enterprises under the leadership of Communist parties'. Using this as an example of Stalin's lack of dialectical method, Mao says that 'Stalin was wrong in rendering absolute the three kinds of ownership'.[30]

However, Mao does not support Khrushchev's accusations against Stalin that the latter called for 'cancellation of commodity production'. Stalin had actually said that commodity production would continue as long as there were two kinds of ownership. Similarly, Mao rejects Khrushchev's insinuation against Stalin that he minimized the law of value in the realm of production, particularly in regard to the role of means of production. Mao says that 'within the framework of ownership by all the people, the buying and selling of means of production do not change ownership'. Moreover, 'the part being played by the law of value in the realm of production is different from what it plays in the process of circulation'. These, according to Mao, are 'virtually consistent' with the viewpoints of Stalin. Mao has a dig at Khrushchev saying that while Stalin objected to selling means of production, such as tractors, to collective farms, Khrushchev sold these things to them.[31]

Thus Stalin's one-sidedness in economic planning and Khrushchev's steps which went further backward have caused tremendous anxieties to Mao. His first major theoretical response to the issue of lopsided development came through the identification of the 'Ten Great Relationships' on April 25, 1956 which stressed the need for dialectically uniting several contending forces like industry and agriculture.[32] Against Stalin's dichotomy between the base and the superstructure, between production and politics, the CPC evolved the policy of 'grasping revolution and promoting production'. And on the most important economic problems of socialism and communism, the Chinese communists have sought to identify the remnants of capitalism in the socialist society on the one hand and the nucleus of communist practice on the other; and have emphasized the need to recognize and restrict the former while encouraging the latter. The Cultural Revolution campaign in China to restrict bourgeois rights had come as an extension of the theory of continuing revolutionary class struggle during the entire period of socialism. It sought to grapple with all these problems of production and superstructure.

On the Method of Discriminating Evaluation

In spite of his 'metaphysics', 'overlord' work-style and economic blunders, Stalin continues to be respected in China. In the national conferences portraits of Marx, Engels, Lenin and Stalin are put up along with, of course, a large portrait of Mao. Stalin's *Problems of Leninism* is included in the currently recommended list of Marxist classics for serious study throughout the country. All this means that what the *Polemic* article stated on the assessment of Stalin still holds good: '... his merits outweighed his faults. He was primarily correct, and his faults were secondary... it is necessary to safeguard what was primary in Stalin's life, to safeguard Marxism-Leninism which he defended and developed.'[33] The article continues : '... it would be beneficial if the errors of Stalin, which were only secondary, are taken as historical lessons so that the communists of the Soviet Union and other countries might take warning and avoid repeating those errors or commit fewer errors.' This is what the Chinese communists seem to be desperately trying to do.

This perspective of avoiding the errors has been explained by Mao in an interesting manner. He says that this is like the pupil trying to excel the teacher. Mao narrates an incident of June 1949 in Moscow. When Stalin toasted China at a banquet for surpassing the Soviet Union in the future, the leader of the Chinese delegation hesitated to drink. Then Stalin said: 'If the pupil cannot surpass the teacher, he is not a good pupil.'[34] At the same time Mao does not like the feeling of inferiority or the notion of 'backward east'. In a speech in 1958 Mao stated: 'In the past, the relations between the Soviet Union and us were those between, father and son, cat and mouse, and the thinking was inflexible. Now it is somewhat better.'[35]

Mao constantly calls for development of knowledge out of one's own experience. He says: 'We lacked understanding of the whole economic situation and understood still less the economic differences between the Soviet Union and China. So all we could do was to follow blindly. Now the situation has changed.'[36] At several places Mao compares and contrasts the Chinese and Soviet conditions to generate appropriate policies and stop uncritical import of ideas. In the years of 'blind faith' Stalin's air of superiority caused considerable discomfort to Mao: 'When heroes and warriors appear on the stage they are made to look quite unlike ordinary people. Stalin was that kind of person. The Chinese people had got so used to being slaves that they seemed to want to go on. When Chinese artists painted pictures of me together with Stalin, they always made me a little bit shorter, thus blindly knuckling under to the moral pressure exerted by the Soviet Union at that time.'[37]

All this provides ample food to psychoanalysts like Erik Erikson. In fact, his analytical tools have been applied by Robert Tucker in a recent study of Stalin suggesting that clues to his political terror could be found in Stalin's early childhood encounters.[38] But appreciation of the political phenomenon of Stalinist errors in a socio-historical perspective has somehow eluded the scholars.[39] The Chinese communist writings have not yet offered a sufficiently researched, theoretically coherent and factually documented study of Stalin. Yet they seem to have identified the correct approach to the problem and to certain of its main aspects.

The most important question that comes to mind when one observes Mao's pen-portrait of Stalin is whether the method of discriminating and critical appreciation of revolutionary leaders can be universally applied. The answer to this seems to be positive. A Marxist should try to see both the correct and the incorrect sides of even Trotsky, Khrushchev, Liu Shaoqi and Lin Biao. However, this method necessarily requires determining the primary side. If the erroneous side is primary and the errors are rooted in the ideology of the overthrown classes, then the denunciation of the leader is total. One may point out that none of the correct aspects of the denounced leaders like Liu Shaoqi and Lin Biao have been mentioned in the Chinese press in recent years. In fact, their errors have been traced as far back as was possible. Without judging the validity of the retrospective accusations, one can say that this is a method of propaganda campaign seriously to bring home the erroneous side.

Mao's appreciation of Stalin generally applies the Marxist notion about the role of leaders in history. On this Mao says: '... the question at issue is not whether or not there should be a cult of the individual, but rather whether or not the individual concerned represents the truth [or the objective trend in history]. If he does, then he should be revered. If truth is not present even collective leadership will be no good.'[40] During the Cultural Revolution when the cult of Mao came into being in China, Mao himself felt uneasy. Soon after the Ninth Party Congress he initiated a campaign against the 'genius theory'. Yet the Chinese political practice, especially initiation of major policies and large-scale campaigns have depended heavily on Mao. Until the socialist revolutionary mode of politics becomes the established pattern in China—the Lin Biao episode showed that it is not yet so—dependence on Mao remains a weak link in China's political development. Therefore, the danger of drifting towards Stalinist errors now or after the death of Mao cannot be altogether ruled out. The dialectical approach suggests that Mao also has both strong and weak points. Currently he seems to be 'representing the truth' and therefore is basically correct. In the past, however, he has been either a willing or an unwilling party to many errors in practice. The major struggles within the CPC objectively reveal both the dimensions of Mao. What implication does this have for evaluating a leader's role in history? The only tentative answer seems to be that the appreciation of a leader is conditioned by both objective and subjective factors. The environment in which the appreciation is undertaken decides its own historical standards. This is the objective element.

Subjectively, the contemporary leader who wants to observe another leader in history has his own dispositions affecting his assessment. (This is true also of observers in general.) If the subjective element is dominant and the objective standard secondary, then the appreciation is more likely to be one-sided. On the whole, Mao, while wishing to look as tall as Stalin, has drawn a picture of Stalin primarily with an eye on the future.

NOTES

1. Mao Tse-tung, 'The Great Friendship', People's China, No. 6 (March 16, 1953).
2. The main body of materials is available in the two-volume mimeographed translations in JPRS, Nos. 61269-1 and 2 entitled *Miscellany of Mao Tse-tung Thought* (MMT), containing selected items from two Chinese language volumes, *Mao Tse-tung Ssu-hsiang Wan-sui*, published in China in 1967 and 1969 during the Cultural Revolution. Other published sources are Stuart Schram (ed.), *Mao Tse-tung Unrehearsed* (Penguin, 1974). See Schram's 'Introduction' for a comprehensive list of the new materials, pp. 53-5. See also Jerome Ch'en, Mao Papers (Bombay: O.U.P., 1971).
3. *The Polemic on the General Line of the International Communist Movement* (Peking: Foreign Language Press, 1965), pp. 122-3.
4. *Mao Tse-tung Unrehearsed*, op. cit., p. 101.
5. Khrushchev, however, called this discriminatory attitude hypocrisy. He says in his memoirs: 'Mao Tse-tung has always been a master at concealing his true thoughts and intentions. Why, I remember after the Twentieth Party Congress, Mao said, "Comrade Khrushchev has opened our eyes and given us light that we might see. He has told us the truth at last. We will reform." But I was always on guard with him. I could tell when he was wheedling us"'. Edward Crankshaw (ed.), *Khrushchev Remembers* (Boston: Little, Brown & Co., 1970), p. 462.
6. *Mao Tse-tung Unrehearsed*, op. cit., p. 102.
7. Ibid., pp. 102-3.
8. 'On the Question of Stalin', op. cit., p. 123.
9. 'Talk on Problems of Philosophy', (August 18, 1964), MMT II, p. 388.
10. Milovan Djilas, *Conversations with Stalin* (New York: Harcourt, Brace & World, 1962), p. 182.

11. 'The Great Friendship', op. cit., p. 4.
12. 'On the Question of Stalin', op. cit., p. 121.
13. 'Interjections at Conference of Provincial and Municipal Committee Secretaries (Collected) (January 1957)', MMT I, pp. 49-50.
14. 'Examples of Dialectics (Abstracted Compilation) (1959)', MMT I, p. 206.
15. 'Speech at the Second Session of the Eighth Party Congress (May 20, 1958)', MMT I, p. 115. See also p. 105.
16. 'Summary of Conference of Provincial and Municipal Committee Secretaries (January 1957)', MMT I, p. 57.
17. 'Speech at the Conference of Heads of Delegations to the Second Session of the 8th Party Congress (May 18, 1958)', MMT I, 121.
18. 'Speech at the Hankow Conference (April 6, 1958)', MMT I, p. 87. Italics added.
19. 'Examples of Dialectics (Abstracted Compilation) (1959)', MMT I, p. 218.
20. 'Summary of Conference of Provincial and Municipal Committee Secretaries (January 1957)', MMT I, pp. 57-8.
21. Richard Levy, 'New Light on Mao: His Views on Soviet Union's Political Economy', *China Quarterly*, No. 61 (March 1975). Levy sees what he calls a 'Timing Theory' of development emerging out of the pages of the new materials. Actually, choice of strategy and policy according to the particular stage of the revolution has always been clear in the Chinese communist practice. Western scholars, however, have not yet taken theoretical formulations concerning people's democratic and socialist revolutions seriously, especially the process of transformation–construction, consolidation, transformation again.
22. MMT I, p. 129.
23. MMT I, p. 161.
24. MMT I, p. 136.
25. 'We must not follow the example of the Soviet academicians who give no attention to the internal contradictions among people.'– 'Speech at Hankow Conference (April 6, 1958)', MMT I, p. 85.
26. MMT I, p. 75.
27. MMT I, p. 130.
28. Ibid.
29. MMT I, p. 144.

30. 'Examples of Dialectics (Abstracted Compilation) (1959?)', MMT I, p. 209.
31. 'Reading Notes on the Soviet Union's "Political Economy"' (1961-2), MMT II, p. 298.
32. *Mao Tse-tung Unrehearsed*, op. cit., pp. 61-83.
33. 'On the Question of Stalin', op. cit., p. 121.
34. 'Speech at the Second Session of the Eighth Party Congress (May 17, 1958)', MMT I, p. 101.
35. 'Speech at the Hankow Conference (April 6, 1958)', MMT I, p. 87.
36. 'Talks at Chengdu', *Mao Tse-tung Unrehearsed*, op. cit., p. 99.
37. Ibid. Italics added.
38. *Stalin as Revolutionary, 1879-1929: A Study in History and Personality* (New York: Norton and Co.), 1973.
39. A new volume which is more factual than earlier accounts of Stalin is Adam B. Ulam, *Stalin: The Man and His Era* (New York: Viking Press, 1973).
40. *Mao Tse-tung Unrehearsed*, op. cit., p. 100.

3

Mao, Deng and Beyond: Dialectics of Early Stage of Socialism

Did China complete the transition from people's democracy to socialism? Mao's emphatic answer was in the affirmative after 1958. Deng had reluctantly agreed with Mao in the early sixties. But thereafter he like Liu Shaoqi and some others, increasingly felt that the transition was not yet complete and it would take a long period to accomplish the tasks of the new democratic stage of the revolution. On this plank he was able to mobilize support in the party after Mao's death, assumed the commanding role and guided the formulation and implementation of a whole range of new policies on every front since the Third Plenum in December 1978.

Compared with the perspective and policies of Mao the new course in China is a historical retreat. But Deng argues that this is a necessary step in order to create the material conditions for socialist construction. It should be noted that the theoretical formulations of the new course are not frankly stated in the language of new democracy lest this retreat appears too obvious. They are justified often in the framework of socialist construction with studious efforts to incorporate new democratic elements into them.[1] In fact, while the policy package of the new course has crystallized in practice, the theoretical explanations have not emerged equally clearly. I shall argue that even though the relative success of the new policies has indicated certain limitations of Mao's political line on socialist construction the retreat towards new democracy is bound to generate new tensions which can be handled by yet newer formulations. They would be inspired both by Mao and Deng. China's struggle for socialist transition is a dialectical process, though a zig-zag one, which creates its own driving forces pulling in different directions at the same time. Just as there was an evolution of policies within the proclaimed line of Mao there is a steady process of policy adjustment within the present-day perspective. But Deng's fundamental break with Mao's line is unmistakable. The new policies are evidently popular in China. But the problems which are likely to arise from this phase will most probably warrant a new response after Deng.

For a New Methodology

The perspective of dialectics of socialist transition avoids several dichotomies which have been used to analyse post-Mao policies in the first half of 1980s. To list a few, some regard Mao as an ideologue and Deng as a pragmatist, Mao as an extremist and Deng as a moderate.[2] Critics of Deng regard him as a revisionist, while critics of Mao regard him as a left dogmatist.[3] Such characterizations are too simplistic.

Undoubtedly both Mao and Deng are ideological in so far as they hold on to their own notions of Marxism. Both exhibited enormous flexibility from time to time. Mao's essay on practice is a treatise on pragmatism. His theory and practice of people's democracy was a pragmatic method of uniting a broad spectrum of people for the anti-colonial and anti-feudal revolution. Even after the Great Leap Forward Mao was a party to pragmatic economic policies during the period 1960-64. It is true that the Cultural Revolution was an ideological upsurge for which Mao bore the main responsibility. But after 1969 he initiated a series of pragmatic steps to counter Lin Biao's influence. Beginning with 1972 he gave a free hand to Zhou Enlai to reintroduce pragmatic measures in the economy and rehabilitate the cadres purged during 1966-69. Even when the Gang of Four was at the height of its power, Mao saw to it that Zhou was re-elected Premier at the Fourth NPC in 1975 with Deng as a Vice-Premier. The policies of agricultural modernization formulated under the leadership of Hua Guofeng in 1975, much to the irk of Jiang Qing, were very different from the line of the Dazhai model, though it was a part of the 'Learn From Dazhai' campaign. Above all in foreign policy Mao demonstrated along with Zhou a high degree of pragmatism from 1969 onwards, though he could not be absolved from the 1967 spell of ultramilitancy in China's foreign policy. Thus, to argue that Mao was a pragmatist till 1957 or 1965 and was a dogmatic idealist after 1966 does not stand to reason.[4]

Deng has been as ideological as Mao a pragmatist. It is known that Deng represented the CPC viewpoint effectively in the ideological discussions with the CPSU. During the first five years of reforms, Deng's ideological approach is evident in almost all spheres. The new economic policies were advanced in terms of Marxist economic laws through the writings of a number of scholars like Hu Qiaomu and Xue Muqiao. A well-organized campaign to weed out the ideological influence of the Gang of Four was launched in 1983 in the form of a party consolidation drive.[5] Deng has made important ideological pronouncements at critical points whenever there was a danger of the new policies going astray. The 1979 proclamation of adherence to the four fundamental principles—Socialist Road, Communist Party leadership, Marxism-Leninism and Mao Zedong Thought, and Dictatorship of the Proletariat—was one such ideological push. The campaign against spiritual pollution launched in 1983 was another, to name a few.

Both Mao and Deng are masters of strategy. They knew that effective strategy synthesizes ideology with practice in the environment. Both are ideological and pragmatic at the same time.

It is equally facile to categorize Mao as an extremist and Deng as a moderate. Extremist or moderate in relation to whom? Mao has been ruthless towards his enemies in the Party, but perhaps not in the way Stalin was. Deng has taken no chances either. After 1978 a series of purges took place in China to remove Deng's critics from office. They included persons like Wang Dongxing, who had frustrated the coup attempt of the Gang of Four and arrested them in October 1976. Both also have some record of sparing their opponents to live in peace or reconciling with them. As to whether a certain policy is moderate or extremist depends on one's own standpoint.

How do the political lines of Mao and Deng fare when put to the test of Marxism-Leninism? In answering this question we encounter several problems arising out of the tradition of polemics in the international communist movement. The debate on revisionism had a positive role in cautioning the ruling communist parties about the dangers of regression. But we also saw easy recourse to trading of charges between 'left deviationists' and 'right opportunists' without always engaging in serious investigation. The methodology of assessing Marxist lines and policies is yet to be fully developed.[6]

The debate on the correct line can perhaps be better conducted in the framework of dialectics of socialist transition. Once there is an adequate appreciation of the contradictions in the early stage of socialism, we can assess various alternative ways of handling them. In course of the search for alternative lines we can apply certain criteria to judge whether a particular line is taking a society further on the socialist path or not. If not, then it is revisionism.

Dialectics of the Early Stage of Socialism

The debate on socialist transition has been intensified in recent years in the context of assessing the new course of development in China. This debate has brought into focus the complex issues which a socialist system has to grapple with in the early years after the seizure of power.

But it is perhaps necessary to put this debate in the perspective of new forces which confront the leadership in socialist countries. The three forces which we can easily identify are: growing mass consciousness, the imperatives of modern technology and self-adjusting mechanism of advanced capitalism. Development strategy today has to reckon with these three forces in all countries including the socialist countries. When problems arising out of these forces are tackled in the context of socialist transition we find new dimensions of the dialectics of the early stage of socialism. Mao and Deng have presented two alternative sets of responses to these problems. I wish to argue that Mao's response attempted a break with the capitalist framework of the industrial revolution. Deng's model was essentially a critique of Mao—valid in parts but operating within the framework of the industrial revolution. For this purpose he has appropriately steered China virtually back to the stage of a people's democratic state. But the very same forces may redirect the course of China's development in the socialist direction, not restoring Mao's path but following a yet newer path inspired by Mao's perspective and Deng's corrective.

This interpretation differs from the viewpoints of Charles Bettelheim on the one hand and the contemporary Chinese scholars like Hu Qiaomu on the other. While the former's arguments amount to a position of political determinism, the latter's line of thought can be described as productionism. It is necessary to work towards a new political economy of socialist transition that reaffirms the original stress by Marx on the *transitional* character of this period, and at the same time comes to grips with the *new problems* of the early stage. This is important in view of the fact that all socialist systems have experienced a process of regression in various degrees.

The Great Proletarian Cultural Revolution (GPCR) in China raised several key issues in the debate on socialist transition. It exposed the weakness in the Soviet pattern of socialist transition by suggesting that the Soviet model did not break with the framework of the industrial revolution. Stalin's goal was to achieve a high degree of industrial development through the mode of public ownership and planned economy. Khrushchev went a step further and introduced elements of market economy.

Mao Zedong in his *Critique of Soviet Economics* pointed out that the Soviet experience failed to bring about the transition towards communism.[7] Whether one agrees with the politics of the GPCR or not, it can hardly be questioned that this campaign drew attention to the decisive criterion of socialist transition, i.e. whether a socialist state can overcome the constraints of capitalist industrial revolution or not. Mao made a determined bid for this. Deng, like Stalin, thought that a socialist state must first achieve the fruits and possibilities of the industrial revolution. Hence their stress on production with the help of technology and management.

The GPCR has influenced the worldwide debate on socialist transition. Charles Bettelheim, commenting on the developments in Poland and Czechoslovakia in the late 1960s, said that the primary fact to be seen in a socialist society was whether the proletariat was effectively exercising its dictatorship and the class struggle was carried out on all fronts. Arguing with Paul Sweezy, he pointed out that it was not enough to base one's judgement on the expansion of market forces in a socialist society or material incentives or location of control of the enterprises in the enterprises.[8] To Bettelheim the loss of power by the proletariat to a new bourgeoisie was the crucial test for determining whether a socialist system was degenerating into capitalism. Sweezy raised the question, how to judge loss of power by the proletariat while agreeing that socialism was more than state ownership and planning. He conceded that the latter might also produce a highly stratified society unless there were other safeguards.

This inconclusive debate between Bettelheim and Sweezy took a new turn after the ushering in of the new course in post-Mao China. Bettelheim described the Chinese development as a 'Great Leap Backward' suggesting that a new bourgeoisie had seized political power in China and had inaugurated a process of capitalist restoration.[9] The *Monthly Review* editors after a period of hesitation came out in 1979 with a refutation of the economic theories underlying the new policies. They did not go as far as Bettelheim, but admitted that a new ideology might be emerging in China.[10] There was a barrage of questions addressed to Bettelheim and most of his critics sought to reconcile the new policies with Mao's experiments at various points of time and refused to accept the Bettelheim scenario. Actually for them the policies of 1977-78, i.e. during the Hua Guofeng interlude were indicators of the new course. When these policies were discarded (on the plea that they carried influences of Mao's 'left' errors), an altogether new line unfolded under Deng's leadership. Thus the exchanges between Bettelheim and his critics are somewhat dated.[11] But it gave enough warnings about the direction in which the wind was blowing.

The victorious line in post-Mao China represented an alternative political economy. Hu Qiaomu provided the theoretical setting in his speech to the State Council in 1978 which was later published under the title 'Observe Economic Laws: Speed Up Four Modernizations'.[12] Later a host of books and articles appeared in the Chinese press including leading contributions by Sun Yefang and Xue Muqiao.[13]

Hu Qiaomu asserts that there are objective economic laws which must be observed by the planners in a socialist system. Violating them would be committing the error of subjectivism. The suggestion was that Mao Zedong's political economy violated these economic laws. Hu identifies three such laws: (i) the law of planned, proportionate development of the national economy; (ii) the law of value; (iii) the law of identity of the interests of the state, the production unit and the individual. There have been different formulations of these laws by different Chinese writers. Xue Muqiao, for example, starts with the law that the relations of production must conform with the level of the growth of productive forces. Secondly, he shows how what Stalin called basic economic law of socialism operates fully in communism and has only restricted application in socialism. This refers to, in Stalin's words, 'the securing of the maximum satisfaction of the constantly rising material and cultural requirements of the whole people...'. Thirdly, Xue talks about continuous operation of the law of value in socialist society due to the persistence of commodity economy. Unlike in capitalism, this is, however, regulated by state planning. In the fourth place Xue talks about the laws peculiar to the period of socialism like the principle of wages determination, 'each according to his work'.[14]

There are differences in nuances between Hu Qiaomu and Xue Muqiao which would make an interesting study in itself. Hu was presenting a critique of both Stalin and Mao in the middle of 1978, whereas Xue, writing after the Third Plenum, criticizes the Hua Guofeng line of achieving high targets. But both the scholars and others were essentially advancing three arguments in defence of 'high standard modernization of the national economy'. Firstly, market forces operate in a socialist society and the state should respect the interplay of these forces rather than ignore them. Second, the individual worker and his/her unit of family or enterprise can work to the best of their ability mainly on the assurance of material rewards. Third, a degree of competition among them was desirable to get the best out of them even though it might lead to inequalities in the short run. All this was permissible in the early stage of socialism for the sake of developing the productive forces which were still low in China. The leadership of the Communist Party and the dominant position of the public ownership system provided enough safeguards to maintain the socialist system. This is how the advocates of the new course defend their perspective on socialist construction.[15]

A 1974 treatise on political economy published from Shanghai sought to present Mao's line of thought and that has obviously come under severe attack in China. It is alleged to have violated the objective economic laws.[16]

The debate on the nature of the dialectics of early socialism will continue. We can only point out the inadequacy of the parameters of the debate. Bettelheim seems to exaggerate the capacity of the political forces when he says that the continuation of class struggle can ensure the development towards communism. Dialectical and historical materialism entails a level of interaction and correspondence between the forces of production and relations of' production, between economy and politics. Within that framework revolutionary politics can accelerate the process of change by developing the forces of production. Betteleheim's interpretation amounts to advocating from the standpoint of political determinism which sees the driving force of change in politics rather than in political economy.

On the other hand, Hu Qiaomu and others like him reduce political economy to production of goods and subordinate the goals of socialist transition to the needs of production. The essence of the socialist transition as explained by Marx in his *Critique of the Gotha Programme* is to create conditions for making the workers control the fruits of their labour.[17] For this the differences between town and country and mental and physical labour should steadily decline. If the worker is subjected to the market forces and inequalities persist, then it is not a transition towards communism.

The Chinese economists have validly criticized the ultra-left tendency of pushing towards equalitarianism even at the cost of productive forces. But Marxist theory postulates the notion of social possibility of a stage of development and a steady movement to realize that possibility.[18] According to this logic, inequalities should gradually decline, however slow the pace may be. Thus the dialectics of stages entail neither an exaggerated leap towards equality nor a stagnation and surely not increasing inequality. On this score political economy of China's new course is somewhat regressive. Its initial value lay in providing a critique of Mao's excessive emphasis on politics. But as an alternative political economy it falls short of fulfilling the norms of socialist transition.

New Forces

The retreat from the phase of socialist construction to the new democratic stage may be an ideological compromise, but it is an alternative response to the problems of the early stage of socialist transition. During this stage there are not only the vestiges of the old system, the threats of the overthrown classes, and the constraints of underdeveloped production as anticipated by Marx and further elaborated by Lenin, there are also some new forces in operation as has been evident during the second half of the 20th century. The debate on socialist transition has by and large been preoccupied with the former set of issues. It is suggested here that the new forces should be comprehended with equal care so that we can properly assess policy and practice in socialist countries. These forces acquire significance as a revolutionary society seeks to realize its ideological goals while facing the challenges of the modern times.

The growth of political consciousness among the masses is the first major force. When revolution takes place through a process of mass struggle or when an elite group seizes political power; in either case the masses get mobilized. Their political and economic hopes are aroused. Politically they may demand greater participation in one form or another. Even more important is the expectation that socialist revolution would bring food, work and prosperity to the masses as promised by the ideology of the revolutionaries. That is seen as the first step towards workers' self-determination. In various ways through initial policy measures, political propaganda and symbolic gestures these hopes are kept alive.

How does a socialist regime respond to this phenomenon of mass consciousness? The Soviet answer under Stalin was that people must make sacrifices to defend the first socialist state against the imperialist threat. So there was an enormous stress on saving for industrialization and defence production rather than for agricultural development and people's welfare. Politically a strong central leadership was justified. The strategy was successful in defending the Soviet state and building the USSR into a leading industrial power.[19] Under Khrushchev the political process was liberalized and more attention was paid to agriculture and consumer welfare. But socialist values were no longer central to mass consciousness. A patriotic commitment to manage the Soviet society efficiently and defend Soviet power internationally has become paramount in the citizens' consciousness in the USSR.

The Chinese revolution was a protracted mass struggle involving a peasant army. People's consciousness had been aroused immensely in course of the national war of resistance against Japan. The CPC was the bearer of the mantle of an agrarian and nationalist revolution. To respond to this situation the CPC leadership debated various strategies during the mid-1950s. While one group of leaders like Liu Shaoqi and Deng Xiaoping argued in favour of continuing the strategy of the First Five Year Plan, Mao opted for a new strategy of all-round development based on mass mobilization. The economic model of the Great Leap Forward was based on mass mobilization. Even though it was a failure, Mao pursued that line of thinking which culminated in the GPCR. Mao's approach was to rely on mass consciousness and turn it into an economic force.[20] As in the Soviet Union, the people were asked to make sacrifices for the growth of industry. But they were to be directly involved in developing industry and agriculture. To carry out this process of mass-line development the CPC was called upon to rely on mass campaigns to arouse people's enthusiasm. In this process the goals of the socialist revolution, particularly the objective of reducing the three great differences while developing productive forces, were to be constantly emphasized.

Liu and Deng found some serious lacunae in this approach to handling mass consciousness. They pointed out that the overall performance of the Chinese economy could have been much better but for Mao's economic policies. Moreover, people's standard of living had been nearly frozen since the mid-1960s. Finally, political mobilization through frequent mass campaigns did not allow socialist institutions and laws to stabilize, and in fact they often led to anarchy, arbitrariness and lawlessness. Therefore, Mao's approach was not enough to generate enthusiasm among the people and sustain their faith in socialism while developing the productive forces at the same time. Deng's new political economy is based upon this critique of Mao.

One of the major factors in the growth of production is technology. When a socialist system of ownership is established the question arises as to how technology should be harnessed so that productive forces arise and people's demands are fulfilled. Lenin had dramatically emphasized this aspect by describing communism as Soviets plus electrification. The Soviet leadership stressed the pre-eminence of technology which fitted well with their model of development. The Chinese communists debated the issue of 'cooperativization first, or mechanization first' in the mid-1950s highlighting the alternative political uses of technology. Mao's initial impulse was to resist the penetration of high technology lest it caused political inequality, unemployment and alienation and was taken as a panacea for underdevelopment. The socialist structure was more important than technology, Mao stressed. Hence came the collectivization of agriculture. But Mao again considered the question of technology during the 1960s and argued that he was not against high technology or import of foreign technology, but wanted to ensure that technology led to self-reliance and socialist development. But this is easier said than done. The closed-door policy on technology has been attributed to the Gang of Four and was severely criticized by the advocates of the new course in China. China now imports sophisticated technology from foreign countries. In addition, post-Mao planners think that new technology must be accompanied by modern scientific management system. The Chinese have introduced several practices borrowed from the Japanese and US systems of corporate management. The Maoist emphasis on workers' participation in management along the lines of the 1960 Anshan Charter is now dismissed as anarchistic, unaccountable and inefficient.

The imperatives of technology are growing every day and no development planner can ignore them. The alternative responses of Stalin, Mao and Deng demonstrate the complexity of reconciling technology with socialist politics. At a time when a worldwide debate is going on regarding the political and cultural consequences of technology, the issue cannot be closed with a simple answer.

The challenge to socialist construction is further confounded by the self-adjusting experience of the advanced capitalist countries. They have faced crisis after crisis, but have come out with new ways of coping with them. The structure of the capitalist system has undergone several reforms in order to maintain its internal efficacy and international power. The world economy remains dominated by the capitalist states because of their capital assets, technology and financial capacity. Hence it is extremely difficult to keep off the pressures of the world capitalist system. Stalin might have succeeded in insulating the Soviet economy but at a great cost. Khrushchev opened up to the West, but from a position of some strength as an industrial power. Mao made self-reliance a creed of national development since the Great Leap Forward. Patriotism was mobilized to support this strategy and a whole range of policies was designed accordingly.

The cost of isolation had to be assessed. Deng pointed out

that it deprived China of access to advanced technology in the world. Now the policy has changed. China could recently buy steel and oil exploration technology from Japan and other technologies from wherever they were available. China's light industry produced textiles, electronics, processed food and other goods which needed a market abroad especially in the Western countries. These industries provided employment to a larger number of workers. At the same time China needed capital to utilize its own natural resources and labour power. Thus China swiftly decided to enter into the world political economy knowing fully well that it is dominated by the advanced capitalist countries. It wanted to take full advantage of this. Of course, within that framework China joins other developing countries in creating pressures on the advanced countries to change the unequal world economic order. At home the leadership also aims at absorbing foreign technology and curb dependence on foreign powers. China's response to the capitalist-dominated world system is parallel to Soviet behaviour. They, too, seek Japanese and western technology and capital from time to time.

The dilemma, therefore, is how to build a self-reliant socialist economy and at the same time promote production on world standards. If the Maoist path is followed, there may be a long-drawn technological disparity between the socialist and the capitalist countries. If there is full-scale integration with the world economy along the new course in China, then not only is dependence on foreign interest increased but capitalist economic practices may be introduced in a Socialist country.

The growth of the foreign and Chinese joint sector in China and the free economic zones bordering Hong Kong and Macao may be channels of foreign capitalist penetration into China. The present leadership assures that the socialist framework is strong enough to contain them. But the craze for foreign goods in China, applications to study abroad and manifestation of Western outlook among the Chinese youth are already a cause for concern among the Chinese leaders. The launching of the campaign against spiritual pollution in 1983 was an official recognition of this problem.[21]

These three new forces—the growth of mass consciousness, the imperatives of modern technology and the pressures of the world capitalist system—are related to each other. Mao tried to grapple with these problems while trying to overcome the framework of the capitalist industrial revolution. That is why he stressed the need to continue the class struggle throughout the socialist period.[22] This political perspective was meant to handle the dialectics of the stage of early socialism and develop into the next stage of maturity. The objective was to involve the masses in politics and development improving workers' welfare but also saving for investment. Technology was to serve political goals rather than operate with full autonomy. Both these measures would discreetly interact with the world economy, again keeping the socialist goals in view.

Deng and his group have discarded the above reasoning, saying that China would remain indefinitely backward and the Chinese rather poor in that scheme of socialist construction. Hence they thought that in order to tackle these problems urgently there was no harm in operating within the framework of new democracy which existed in the early 1950s. That was based on the concept of a united front of workers, peasants and petit and national bourgeosie. It would unite the whole country for accomplishing the task of development. This approach would also appeal to the people in Taiwan, Hong Kong and Macao besides touching the soft chord in the hearts of overseas Chinese and people in the West. United efforts and all-out mobilization for modernization that is the theme of post-Mao China. The framework of new democracy allows a degree of political and organizational freedom to non-communist groups which they welcome very much.

Is the new course in China an adequate response to the dialectics of the early stage of socialism? The tentative hypothesis outlined here suggests the contrary. Mao Zedong's political economy was not adequate either. But it had alerted socialist systems to the magnitude of the problems of socialist construction. Deng's alternative contains a valuable critique. Therefore, the problems facing China require fresh responses.

NOTES

1. As against the PRC Constitutions of 1975 and 1978, which had described China as a 'Socialist State of the Dictatorship of the Proletariat', the 1982 Constitution describes it as a 'Socialist State Under the People's Democratic Dictatorship' (Article 1). In his Report to the Twelfth Party Congress in 1982, Hu Yaobang called for doing 'everything possible to strengthen the broadcast patriotic united front' and referred to the role of the democratic parties under socialism.
2. Mao himself assumed the role of a 'moderate' in his criticism against the political line of Lin Biao during 1970-71 and of Jiang Qing in 1974-75.
3. Much of the Western journalistic commentary on post-Mao policies has taken the easy recourse to this line of analysis describing them as pragmatic.
4. Mao's alleged dogmatism after 1966 was sometimes explained in psychoanalytic terms as by Lucien Pye, *The Man in the Leader* (New York: Basic Books, 1976).
5. 'Decision on Party Consolidation', *Beijing Review*, vol. 26, no. 42, October 17, 1983.
6. To formulate a new mothodology for analysing shifts in socialist system we have to keep three things in mind, namely, that two-line struggle is more than a personalized conflict, that there is a continuous gap between policy and practice and that single events have to be placed within an understanding of the primary process going on in a society. See my 'Assessing Chinese Developments', *Frontier*, May 31, 1980. For an interesting comment on this see Rabin, 'Assessing China', *Frontier*, September 13, 1980. The changes in China have indeed affected the primary process in the society.
7. Mao criticized Stalin's strategy of economic development as 'walking on one leg'. See Mao Zedong, *A Critique of Soviet Economics* (New York: Monthly Review Press, 1977). Also my 'Mao's Portrait of Stalin', *China Report*, vol. xi, no. 4, July-August 1975.
8. Paul M. Sweezy and Charles Bettelheim, *On the Transition to Socialism* (New York: Monthly Review Press, 1971), p. 16.
9. Charles Bettelheim, 'Great Leap Backward', *Monthly Review*, vol. 30, nos. 3 and 4, July-August, 1978.
10. Editors, 'China: New Theories for Old', *Monthly Review*, vol. 31, no. 1, May 1979, p. 9.
11. The Hua Guofeng interlude in China had the significance of reconciling the Maoist approach with the tasks of economic

development. After the Third Penum he was criticized for 'left' errors and ambitious plans.

12. Hu Qiaomu, *Observe Economic Laws, Speed Up Four Modernisations* (Beijing: Foreign Languages Press, 1978).
13. Xue Muqiao, *China's Socialist Economy* (Beijing: Foreign Languages Press, 1981).
14. Ibid., pp. 297-307.
15. See, for example, 'A Brief Introduction to Sun Yefang's Economic Theory', *Beijing Review*, vol. 26, no. 24, June 13, 1983.
16. *Fundamentals of Political Economy* (Trans. George Wang) (New York: M.E. Sharpe, 1977). This is the translation of a two-volume work by Writing Group (Shanghai: Shanghai People's Press, 1974).
17. 'Critique of the Gotha Programme' by Karl Marx has been interpreted as an attack on premature egalitarianism by many. But it also points out that the 'lower stage of communism' is a substantial advance over capitalism and paves the way to a higher stage of communism. Marx says, for example, 'the exchange of equivalents in commodity exchange only exists *on the average* and not in the individual case' (italics in the original). Marx and Engels, *Selected Works* in 3 vols. (Moscow: Progress, 1970), p. 18.
18. I have discussed the Marxist concept of equality in 'Towards a Political Theory of Equality' in Andre Beteille (ed.) *Equality and Inequality* (New Delhi: Oxford University Press, 1983). Commenting on the phenomenon of acquiescent socialism, I have suggested that the social possibility of a stage of development has to be correctly discerned and progressively realized.
19. The complexity of the Soviet experience needs to be further probed as argued effectively by Archie Brown, 'Political Power and the Soviet State: Western and Soviet Perspectives' in Neil Harding (ed.) *The State in Socialist Society* (London: Macmillan, 1984).
20. This has been assessed in international perspective by Samir Amin, *The Future of Maoism* (New York: Monthly Review Press, 1983).
21. Deng Liqun explained the problem at a press conference. See *Beijing Review*, vol. 26, no. 45, November 7, 1983.
22. Mao's view on class struggle in socialist society has been rejected by the new leadership. *The Resolution on CPC History (1949-81)* says: 'Class struggle no longer constitutes the principal contradiction after the exploiters have been eliminated as classes.' However, it continues to exist within limits, according to the resolution, as there are hostile elements in society.

4

Between Truth and Revolution: Will China Opt for Detente Social Sciences?

I

The widely welcomed resurgence of social science activity in China has appeared on the world scene at a critical juncture of the history of social sciences. In the post-World War II period the liberal democratic societies presented highly advanced levels of research on social issues. But, as imperialist systems crumbled and the crisis in Western societies deepened, social sciences too, showed cracks in dominant theories, models and methodologies. During the 1960s the social science scene appeared to have been struck by an upheaval.

There were three main streams of response to this upheaval, each of which had one or more counter-trends. In the West the pristine defenders of present-day liberalism asserted relatively more conservative ideas on capitalist development, positivist science, value-free history, pluralist democracy and the like. The challengers of the 1960s remained a small radical stream of thought and a conglomerate that included Marxian utopians as well as classical liberals. In the socialist states of eastern Europe and the Soviet Union the crisis in bourgeois social sciences was noticed, but the new trend of detente survived this interruption. As a result, what may be called a 'detente social science' which was less ideological and more tied to management of industrial society, grew up steadily in these countries. (In 1980 functionalist social science was already more pervasive in Poland and Yugoslavia than in France and West Germany!) Marxist social science has not made matching progress in socialist states as liberal social science has in capitalist states, for various reasons. But this question requires separate treatment.

Detente social science does not apply class analysis to understand social phenomena, nor does it regard ideological differences between social systems as of any major significance to explain the variety of social processes. It is based on the convergence thesis that industrialization is a definite process which goes on in all societies and that they have to come to grips with it in order to become modern and strong. Sometimes it takes the form of a social science that champions the common causes of mankind like peace, world order, human rights and clean environment. Indeed, these are universal concerns of people all over the world, but each of these has its political dimension which only the naive analysts can ignore.

In the third world countries the 1960s also saw intense economic crisis and exposure of the weaknesses of the prevalent development models. It is at this time that in countries like India the inherited social science situation, which was a mix of colonial pattern and traditional mode, was responding to the advanced Western social science trends. Through a variety of interaction between third world educational systems and Western universities, foundations and governmental agencies, new trends developed. The major trend was championed by a set of liberal intellectuals who adopted the dominant Western theories and models and applied them to the third world situation. In some ways they performed the role of comprador academics.[1]

Dominant theories or models representing advanced technology were constructed in Western, chiefly American, academic centres. Collaborating academics in India conducted empirical investigation collecting field data on electoral behaviour and so on. Questionnaires, like raw materials in case of the classical colonial economic practice, were shipped to advanced centres for computer analysis. Final products in the form of powerful theories, well-produced and publicized, came back to swamp the native market. Indigenous academics had no resources in those days to match such massive operations. Their counter response to the modern trend setters in Indian social science had several strands. The conservatives remained more or less unimpressed. The Marxists who were not won over by detente social science rejected them as bourgeois thought systems. As comprador academics faced intense criticism from all sides, a new trend slowly grew out of their self-reflection. This group of scholars asserted a 'third world' dimension to social analysis, pleaded for modification and adaptation of Western social theories and talked about indigenous values of specific cultures and societies which determined their social enquiry. This can be called the neo-liberal campaign in certain circles of third world social sciences, which became an articulate trend in the late 1970s.

The neo-liberal campaign which is one of the dominant trends in India today criticizes positivist science and in the process almost wipes out the scientific method. It attacks the dominant power structures in the world but does not identify itself with anti-imperialist and anti-colonial movements. It claims to relate social science to concrete problems of society without even once attempting to characterize the social nature of the state or the class character of the society. Yet they launch elaborate epistemological plans for alternative development strategies. The neo-liberals' reluctance to attack capitalism has made them happily acceptable to the ruling intellectual circles of the Western countries. The closest the neo-liberals take social science to seeking truth is when they loudly spurn the talk of making social science 'relevant' to society. That kind of abstractification goes well with their critique of positivism. But they are not condemned only to indulge in abstractions. As in Western and socialist systems, the third world social science oligarchs too sit on policy-making bodies whenever politically feasible, and chart out action programmes. When some social scientists of Southeast and West Asia demanded that nationalism be a basic component of social science approaches, Indian neo-liberals were among those who applied the brakes and underlined the universal character of knowledge.[2] The universal character of knowledge is hardly to be disputed. But the question is how to reduce the existing parochialisms imposed by colonialism and neo-colonialism. Therefore, accent on nationalism may in fact facilitate a trend of universalization rather than hinder it.

The relationship between Indian neo-liberal social science and detente social science has been dialectical. On the one hand, the third world orientation implies an aspect of struggle. But, on the other hand, the dentente aspect representing convergence of certain ideas, peaceful cooperation between capitalist and socialist powers and the fact that material support of the superpowers is needed for international dialogue have created an amazingly extensive friendship between the neo-liberals of the third world and the detente social science.

This is the international social science environment today. In the West a functionally modernized liberal orthodoxy prevails basking in the glory of effectively enthroning detente social science in many socialist countries, while in third world countries like India a local variety of bourgeois social science has risen to power. In all cases social science seems to have strayed from its original character of marrying the quest for truth with revolutionary transformation of society. Now the question is whether the Chinese are going to join one of these camps.

II

Social science research in China more or less followed the Soviet pattern during the 1950s and early 60s. During the GPCR the intellectuals were denounced en masse as the condemned ninth category and were branded either as bourgeois democrats or revisionists. Hundreds of them were sent to May 7 cadre schools and other places for extensive terms of labour. Only those intellectuals who supported the GPCR line and advocated the perspective of revolutionary class struggle in every branch of culture were allowed to function.[3] Interaction with foreign social science circles, whether from the West or from the socialist states, was minimal.

After the fall of the Gang of Four and especially since 1978 there has been a great upsurge in social science activity.

Establishment of research institutes, publication of numerous periodicals and books, holding of seminars, exchange of scholars with foreign countries, sending students abroad for higher studies, are indications of this upsurge. In late 1977 the Department of Philosophy and Social Sciences was separated from the Chinese Academy of Sciences and an independent institution called the Chinese Academy of Social Sciences (CASS) was formed. Many old institutes were split into specialized bodies and several new institutes were set up. As of early 1980, there were 22 institutes. Five of them are concerned with the field of economics showing the motivation to orient social sciences towards the programme of four modernizations. They are the Institutes of Economics, Industrial Economy, Agricultural Economy, Finance and Trade and World Economy. There are three institutes in the field of history, two dealing with ancient and modern, and the third with world history. The others are the Institutes of Marxism-Leninism-Mao Zedong Thought, Philosophy, Linguistics, Literature, Foreign Literature, Archaeology, Nationalities, Law, World Politics, South Asia, World Religion, Journalism and Social Science Information. There are some more institutes in the offing. Some of them are in the shape of national academic societies like the Societies of Education, Econometrics, Historical Documents, African Affairs, etc.

In the Chinese system as in the USSR, even though social science institutes are still under one autonomous academy, the institutes are centralized research bodies heavily financed by the state. The best talents are usually located in the institutes, and they may or may not hold concurrent professorships in the universities. In both countries talents from all over the country are centrally located in the capital. Each province also has many institutes, and in China cities like Shanghai, Nanjing and Wuhan can boast of highly rated scholars. Still the concentration of scholarship in the national capital is striking. The institutes directly participate in the policy-making process. In 1980 for example, the Chinese government appointed four committees of economists to formulate proposals for the implementation of the Three-Year Plan of Readjustment and for drafting the

Sixth Five-Year Plan. Two economist vice-presidents of the CASS, Yu Guangyuan and Ma Hong, headed two of these committees. Hu Qiaomu, the CASS president, became a member of the party secretariat which was revived in February 1980. In return for this service to the state the scholars get adequate status, material benefits and facilities to work. But such a close relationship with the state leadership has its own problems to which we will return shortly.

The CASS and other academic institutions have launched a major publication programme. By early 1980 as many as 170 social science journals were being published. Many of them were resumed after a decade's interruption. Some like *Lishi Yanjiu* and *Jinqji Yanjiu* were, however, resumed much earlier in 1972-73. Several new journals appeared on the scene. *Jingji Quanli*, for example, is geared towards discussing Chinese and foreign management systems in the context of the present modernization drive. Beginning in January 1980, a bi-monthly scholarly journal *Zhonqguo Shehui Kexue* started publication under the auspices of the CASS which has a quarterly English edition. The CASS has organized several national and international seminars during that period. A large scale programme of sending Chinese students abroad for higher studies was inaugurated in late 1978, most of the students going to the USA, Canada and West European countries as well as to Japan. Chinese scholars were now participating in many more international conferences than before. (A CASS delegation led by Yang Chengfang, Director, Institute for Social Science Information, took part for the first time in the Third Conference of the Association of Asian Social Science Research Councils held in Manila in September 1979.)

The scholars in Chinese academic institutions today enjoy relatively more freedom and better facilities than in the past. In 1980, I learnt in course of my discussions in China that they are not required to perform manual labour for more than one-fifth of their working time. In some cases there are full exemptions. The administration has been reorganized and the revolutionary committee has been replaced by a single administrative head with a party committee having supervisory power. Ranking of scholars into Professors, Associate Professors, Lecturers and Assistant Lecturers has been reintroduced. The restoration of degrees in colleges was a matter of time. All this reverses the policies of the GPCR which insisted on intellectuals performing manual labour, subjected them to criticism by students and masses and kept them under the control of the revolutionary committees—policies manifestly evoked scornful references by the Chinese intellectuals. The overall policy underlying these measures has many significant implications.

III

A national conference of Party Committee Secretaries from institutes of social sciences was held in the middle of 1980 and it reiterated the policy framework on social science development which had become clear in the course of the two preceding years. Two significant principles underlying the present social science policy have often been identified. Firstly, social scientists are called upon to integrate theory with practice, secondly, the government pursues the policy of 'letting a hundred flowers blossom and a hundred schools of thought contend' towards the intellectuals.[4]

Three corollaries of the first principle have been prominently emphasized. Stressing the social purpose of the social sciences, it is constantly pointed out that social science activity should have the aim of contributing towards social transformation. This takes place in many ways. The writings of the social scientist influence the minds of men. He participates in many action programmes, both helping in the process of the governmental decision-making as well as other non-governmental spheres. Another corollary of the integral relationship between theory and practice is to 'proceed from reality' in understanding and solving problems—reality as it exists rather than reality as it should be. Again and again the leadership points out that any mechanical application of theory or a fixed formula without taking the time period or circumstances of their formulation into full account is likely to do more harm than good. In addition to this, another idea constantly talked about is that 'practice is the sole criterion for testing truth'. Principles which are currently disproved by practice are to be discarded in favour of new principles.

While the above principle spells out the philosophical orientation advocated by the post-Mao leadership for social science work, the method of managing the social science workers, their rights and opportunities is embodied in the 'two hundreds policy'. Let us recall that this policy had triggered off a major campaign of critical discussion in 1957 among the intellectuals, and when the tide of criticism was unmanageable it was withdrawn. The reform leadership which seeks to mobilize the maximum range of non-party forces behind the CPC for carrying out the four modernizations has logically reinvoked this principle. At the intellectual plane too, the idea of free discussion has been defended as creating more possibilities for enriching knowledge. Moreover, the Gang of Four had imposed their ideological and political line on the intellectuals with an iron hand and it had led to the suspension of much of the social science activity. Hence the 'two hundreds policy' has been popularized and put into Article 14 of China's Constitution. Besides, under the newly enforced legal system, intellectuals like others can also avail of the safeguards against political harassment. Excessive interference by party leaders in intellectual activity has been disallowed even though party committees continue to perform supervisory functions in academic institutions.

During the trial of the Gang of Four, framing and persecution of intellectuals were major charges against Yao Wenyuan and Jiang Qing.

Both these principles are unquestionably laudable in themselves. It is necessary to remind the social scientist of this social task at a time when the social scientist in many parts of the world is fast becoming either a small project engineer or a model builder. Simultaneously the need for creative development of ideology and combating dogmatism is always there. The Chinese revolution and post-liberation social reconstruction under Mao Zedong are themselves vindications of these principles. Similarly, the only way to check state-backed social science from degenerating into an exercise in rationalization of the prevailing political line is to ensure that the state encourages debates on basic issues. Hence, the principles proclaimed in China recently are by and large conducive to social science development. But the context, in which these principles have been announced and the way their concrete practice has begun, raise some questions about the directions of their development.

Proceeding from reality and taking practice as the sole criterion of truth are being advanced by the leadership to negate the 'left' deviationist influence of the Gang of Four. The new line has repudiated the theory and the policies of the GPCR including the theory of continuous revolution, taking class struggle as the key link in every sphere, etc. Mao Zedong's ideas on socialist construction, too, have come under criticism and the thesis of the Eighth Party Congress of 1956 has been reiterated. A campaign to emancipate one's mind (*jiefang xixiang*) has been on in China, which implies that people should give up the ideas advanced during the GPCR or even since the Great Leap Forward. In this context the call to take practice as the sole criterion of truth may have come simply to mean 'be pragmatic'.

The dialectical materialist theory of knowledge, especially its law of unity, of knowing and doing, does stress practice as the source of knowledge, practice both in the production process and in the social process. It is through unending practice that perceptual knowledge becomes conceptual and rational knowledge which is constantly enriched through practice. But this is also subject to the law of contradictions, universal as well as particular. To compartmentalize practice and contradictions may reduce the concept of practice to empiricism and the concept of contradictions to dogmatism.[5] In fact some Marxists did level the charge of empiricism against Mao's concept of practice. But if we take the two essays of Mao *On Practice* and *On Contradictions* together and see their interconnection, the two extremes of deviation are avoided and yet enough room is made for creative development of ideology. The contemporary discussion of truth in China talks mainly about the empirical validity of specific principles in specific situations. Truth seems to be equated with validity which is taken as a contingent and not universal category. Seeking truth in science means seeking objective laws of development. The task of social science is to search for truth or objective laws of social development.

The Chinese social scientists do talk about objective economic laws when they point out that these laws were violated by the Gang of Four and possibly by Mao. Both philosophically as well as in the context of specific policies the gang as well as Mao are accused of idealism and subjectivism. But it seems that, just as the search for truth strayed into idealist deviation during the GPCR, there are some indications that the recent orientation might cause a deviation towards empiricism and pragmatism. This could be a period of reaction to the preceding phase—a phenomenon so familiar in Chinese history; but if it is prolonged, then the search for objective laws will be hampered and social planning based on faulty understanding might be faulty.

When the state as well as party authority are rallied behind a dominant philosophical orientation, be it idealist or empiricist, then there are many dangers. Since the tasks of social development are urgent, social scientists are mobilized with patriotic and revolutionary appeals and usually a great intellectual fervour is created. During the GPCR, it was one kind of intellectual upheaval and now another kind, though the vast number of intellectuals now seem genuinely to be energized. In such a situation when one line is replaced by another at the top, there comes a mechanical restandardization. We know from the experience of the Chinese intellectuals in recent decades that many of them just stop working or go to quiet research. Some become experts in service of the new line, and a majority just switch their support. Such experiences are also familiar in India and in a subtle way in the West. There have been Nehru waves and Gandhi waves in India under official patronage, though contradictions in the Indian environment have made any type of standardization difficult. This call for respecting the dominant line for the sake of revolution causing standardization of orientation hampers the search for truth, and it also hinders the capacity of the social scientist to contribute towards social development. It may bring up social science technicians selling their expertise in the market for all kinds of buyers. But in the long run, it inhibits social science development and also social development.

The state has every right to ensure that the social science community respects the goals of the social revolution in an overall sense, but it cannot impose a ruling leadership's interpretation of those goals. The state having a class character is bound to protect and encourage ideas which serve the interest of the classes in power. This is true both of capitalist and socialist states. In socialist states where working class perspectives on research are theoretically encouraged, there must be enough support by the state for the intellectuals to define, debate, and enrich those perspectives. Even a most dedicated leadership committed to national development defeats its purpose by imposing its line for social science activity.

Let us recall what Zhou Yang, China's top cultural authority, spelled out as the fighting tasks in October 1963, i.e. before the GPCR in his famous address to the Department of Philosophy and Social Sciences. His entire thesis was a repudiation of Soviet social science which had developed in the late 1950s and early 1960s, which we have called 'detente social science'. The stress on the class struggle perspective pervaded his speech. Criticizing pragmatism as the ideology of imperialism and the bourgeoisie, Zhou Yang said: 'It holds that truth is nothing but an instrument used by man to achieve his immediate purposes in his acts of coping with the environment and its motto is that "it is true because it is useful." He also called the representatives of modern revisionism the political worshippers of the United States who followed the American brand of pragmatist philosophy. At the same time, Zhou Yang advocated summing up contemporary experiences and creatively applying the theories to concrete situations and also developing the theories.

Zhou Yang, who was a Vice-President of the CASS in 1980s, seemed to have adopted the prevailing line which was very different from his 1963 thinking.

The indications are that the new policies towards social sciences in China have decisively taken a pragmatist turn, in which case they would be in the category of 'detente social science' which has ostensibly no class character and is geared towards problems of modernization in all societies. The kind of value movement, struggle between various ideological lines, and fierce social science debates which characterize the Indian academic scene today and which have largely prevented 'detente social science', from bulldozing Indian academia, are unlikely in the Chinese situation. However, close interacticn with third world social science may expose the Chinese to the various complexities of the development process which are being debated in the third world today. Hence the possibilities open for Chinese social science are either to carry on social science activities within their distinct Marxist framework having open debates and equitable interaction with the world, or to plunge into 'detente social science' availing of the enormously tantalizing collaboration coming from the West. The present international environment favours the latter possibility. Already China has sought the services of Western management experts, lawyers, and other scholars, and numerous exchange programmes with the West have been concluded. The proportion of intellectual interaction with the third world is abysmally small. In this situation, China has started seriously re-evaluating the nature of the Soviet system which was overdue in any case. Still, China's absorption into 'detente social science' may not be easy because of continuing debates on the nature of socialist construction in China. They, too, are likely to 'seek truth from practice', and draw their lessons.

NOTES

1. For a discussion of this concept, see Manoranjan Mohanty, 'The Political Essence of Progress' (paper presented at the International Seminar on Political Development in South Asia held in March 1973 at Rajasthan University, Jaipur).
2. See the proceedings of the seminar on Indigenization of Social Sciences held on the occasion of the Third General Conference of the Association of Asian Social Science Research Councils (AASSRC), Manila, September 12-17, 1979.
3. For a picture of the social science scene during the GPCR, see Krishna Prakash Gupta, "Society as a Factory—Maoist Approach

to Sciences", *China Report*, vol. viii, no. 3, May-June 1972, Delhi.

4. The line was first put forward authentically in Hua Guofeng's 'Report on the Work of the Government' presented to the Second Session of the Fifth NPC in June 1979. A succinct presentation of the broad framework is contained in the country report presented by Yang Chengfang at the AASSRC Conference in 1979, cited above.
5. Implications of the unity of knowing and doing have been explained in Manoranjan Mohanty, *The Political Philosophy of Mao Zedong*, Chapter IV (New Delhi: Macmillan, 1978, 2nd ed., Delhi: Aakar Books, 2012).

5

The Political Economy of Development in PRC at 40: Socialism in the Freedom Scale*

The Intellectual Moment

The 40th anniversary of the founding of the People's Republic of China (PRC) came at a time when the pace of changes in socialist systems surpassed all predictions. Reforms in Poland and Hungary made the Yugoslav experiment seem underdeveloped. The process in these countries predated the Gorbachev reforms; but it no doubt gained momentum by the process of *perestroika* in the USSR. These developments have generated heated debates both within these countries and outside. Within the countries there are the veterans who despise this trend as a deviation from Marxism, and the reformists many of who find the peace of restructuring too slow and meagre. In the Western countries, the liberal democrats find in this development the 'inevitable failure of the socialist experiment' and vindication of capitalism. In the context of the rise of the 'new right', or Thatcherism, this view got wide publicity through the Western media.

In the PRC the debate has been going on since 1960s. Since the Great Leap Forward various groups in the CPC leadership

---

* This essay written on the occasion of the 40th anniversary of the People's Republic of China in 1989 takes up the theoretical issues relating to the agenda of building socialism. The tables have been updated for comparative purposes.

have argued with each other about the nature of socialist transition. The Cultural Revolution was waged by Mao Zedong on the question of quality and pace of transformation and the direction of socialism in China. The Deng Xiaoping regime repudiated Mao's line on socialist construction and unfurled a reforms strategy to achieve the modernization of China. June 1989 saw the explosion of a crisis resulting from the consequences of the reforms decade. Thus, while the people of China should be jubilant for their great achievements during the last four decades, the Tian'anmen episode had clouded the celebration of the victory of the Chinese Revolution. This is so despite the fact that the Deng leadership has reaffirmed its overall strategy of 'reforms and open door'.

Besides the upheavals in the socialist countries, there was an intellectual upsurge in the social sciences in general and in Marxism in particular which arose from the people's movements and social practices touching upon the issues of democracy and human rights, cultural identity and class complexities, the state and social movements—ecology, peace and gender equality being some of the central issues of these movements. These developments have challenged all theoretical systems including Marxism. Since Marxism claimed to scientifically grapple with these issues the debates in Marxist theory, have been more intense, some finding the traditional formulations adequate while others seeking to develop creative theory out of Marxist methodology.

It is at this intellectual moment, one that is characterized by upheavals in the socialist systems, political struggle in China and a new atmosphere of questioning, that we have to grasp the character of the political economy of development in China. Our exercise mainly seeks to identify the principal explanation for the periodic crisis situations in socialist countries despite their many achievements in almost all fields. The periodic crises reflect some old and new contradictions in the course of the development process. Our explanation for these crisis situations is located in the loss of the integral perspective of socialist political economy. The integral perspective refers to simultaneously developing material conditions and political participation—and now we must add cultural creativity—to achieve the socialist goals. We would like to stress the interdependence of the three dimensions. While creation of material conditions is necessary for socialist development, they are not sufficient and their production and distribution are seriously affected by the other two dimensions too. Inadequate realization of their interconnection and enforced imbalances by the implementation of policies by the winning factions of Communist Party leaderships in various countries have caused serious contradictions in socialist practice. The new political economy of socialism has to restore the focus on freedom and seek to explain the process of enlarging the realization of socialist freedom and its setbacks.

From this perspective we shall first examine the debate of the political economy of socialist transition in general and also in the context of China. Then we will assess the trends in the Chinese political economy over the past four decades. Finally, we will return to the discussion of socialist development in the freedom scale and look into the future.

Perspectives on Socialist Transition

Since both 'political economy' and 'development' have acquired wide currency though with very different meanings, it may be in order to provide working definitions of them for the purposes of this essay.

Political economy does not merely refer to political dimensions of economy and economic dimensions of politics even though both these aspects are included in it. Many theorists of growth who identify political conditions conducive or detrimental to growth also loosely use the term political economy. Neither of these views is satisfactory because they see politics and economics as separate processes and political economy does not admit that separation. It is conceived as a process involving both production and the power structure. According to this view, human exploration of nature is constantly interacting with the power structure in society. While political economy as a discipline was accepted by classical economists like Adam Smith and Ricardo, it was left to Marx to apply the class dimension to it. Classical political economy treated the individual as an independent producer and capital as money, tools and raw materials. Marx pointed out that capital was a social relation between owners of means of production and the owners of labour power. The constant struggle between them about the organization of the labour process marked the character of the social environment within which production and distribution go on. Marx argued that changes in the human knowledge on exploration of nature, or change in the forces of production have a decisive effect on the relations of production or the way the owners of the means of production and the rest of the society are organized. This broad approach was applied by Marx to analyse the dynamics of capitalism in the middle of the 19th century. In recent decades the debates on the crisis in capitalism, the labour theory of value and the nature of the capitalist state have added many significant elements to this approach.[1] Together with them, we find the political economy approach as a comprehensive approach to explain the process of social change, the nature of contradictions in the process, character of the stage of development and the possible points of intervention.

Connected with the above statement is our definition of development as movement in the freedom scale. Development is not merely growth of production even though growth is an essential part of it. But growth may not be necessary on all fronts in the same way. Development has also been regarded as a process of multidimensional change in the desired direction. But that keeps it too open. Development as 'empowerment of the deprived sections' is a concept that is gaining currency in the developing countries. But this notion does not relate this aspect with the overall process of change. Since the perspective of the industrial revolution provided the basic meaning to the concept of development involving industrialization, urbanization and technological progress, many theorists have sharply reacted to this view pointing to the authoritarian and alienating effects of 'development' and have rejected the concept itself.[1] But taking the very same criticisms and also the positive assertions of the earlier theorists we can define development in the freedom scale. As mentioned earlier it is a three-dimensional scale involving (a) the generation of material conditions, (b) political participation, and (c) cultural creativity. Such a notion is intrinsically value-oriented. Therefore; for advocates of socialist development, it means movement towards the socialist goals of freedom. This necessarily involves curbing class domination as well as other social dominations based on ethnic, racial, religious and caste divisions as well as patriarchy. Reduction of sources of alienation and increasing conditions of freedom are embedded in the Marxist notion of development as movement towards a classless and stateless society.

We made this definitional digression to place our discussion on socialist political economy in the broader field of the social sciences. Now let us take up the question of socialist transition.

Much of the writings on socialist transition have sought to explain deviations in the process of development in the socialist or communist party-led systems assuming that a policy package could be clearly derived from the writings of Marx and Engels on the transitional phase. On the contrary, the entire field of socialist political economy is based on the practical experience of the socialist regimes themselves. Therefore, by its very character this field is constantly developing and there cannot be a statement of immutable laws of socialist development. Even if Marx had provided a detailed blueprint, it would be dated. We can only discern the method underlying Marx's analysis and apply it to understand and change reality.

Another problem with the existing literature on socialist transition is their preoccupation with 'crisis' in socialist systems to the exclusion of their achievements. At one level this can be explained by the high expectations raised by the revolutions led by communist parties which have not been fulfilled. Hence the leaders and parties are taken to task and charged with revisionism. This is so if the discourse on socialist transition is among Marxists. In non-Marxist circles objectives and performance records are assessed according to their respective criteria or standard indicators which have gained universal currency. In both cases, there is a methodological flaw if their frameworks do not take into account the ideological goals of the revolution and its successes as well as failures.

Khrushchev's reforms in the Soviet Union, the Sino-Soviet dispute and the uprisings in Hungary, Czechoslovakia and Poland had generated a heated debate on the causes of revisionism. The Cultural Revolution in China, the Deng Xiaoping reforms and the Gorbachev wave have focused on structural deficiencies in the prevailing political economy in the socialist systems. For the first set, works of Marx and Engels and the debates in the Soviet Union were reference points. Here the points of comparison are the developed capitalist countries which under Reagan and Thatcher have shown a degree of confidence. But there are problems with both the phases of the debate. In case of the earlier debate on revisionism there was a refusal to admit new elements in the developing environment and an insistent drive to apply historical inferences from Marx and Lenin in almost a parallel way. In case of the prevailing debate on reforms and *perestroika* there is an inadequate emphasis on the historical linkage with the revolutionary process and consequently with the ideological goals of the revolution. It would cause problems because the forces released by the revolution cannot be suppressed easily.

Thus the new political economy of socialist transition has to own the revolution's legacies, apply dialectical materialist methods in a dynamic manner taking into account new forces in the environment and tackle objective problems in society.

Talking about objective problems in a socialist society, Arun Bose identifies five of them which according to him are 'hard facts of life' in socialist societies. (He wrote this in 1975, but the current reforms are actually addressed to these problems among others) They are: (a) bureaucratic waste in socialist planimplementation, (b) the functioning of 'democratic centralism' which invariably gives rise to the personality cult, (c) parasitism or the phenomenon of unproductive labour in the planning process, (d) alienation (in the Marxist sense, of the producer from the product and his/her fellow producers) and, (e) elitist inegalitarianism. How are these problems integrated to provide a key explanation for the character of the overall process? Perhaps politics gives us a clue by taking alienation as the central problem. K.K. Das Gupta has put it thus: 'The reform in the superstructure which aims at transcending the alienation of the party from the masses and that of the state from its citizens to pave the way for a harmonious interaction between the base and the superstructure, has to come from within and not by an overthrow of the present socialist system'.[4]

But curbing alienation and the pursuit of freedom have to involve a comprehensive strategy that answers objective problems in the economy and other spheres. Janos Kornai, who has exposed the 'economics of shortage' in socialist systems, has identified the contradictions in the economy and society and also the dilemma of choice. He believes there are inherent conflicts between efficiency-linked values and the principles of socialist ethics and concludes that 'it is impossible to create a closed and consistent socio-economic normative theory which would assert, without contradiction, a politico-ethical value system and would at the same time provide for the efficiency of the economy. It is impossible if that theory seeks to be realistic and wishes to take into account the true behavioural characteristics of people, communities, organizations and social groups.'[5]

Kornai has depicted the economic behaviour very well in Hungary and other socialist systems and their dysfunctional aspects and has made a case for practical compromises between the two sets of principles. But his suggestions sound more like economic realism derived from the experiences of capitalist countries than one that is based on socialist political economy.

The centrality of the political question was highlighted by Charles Bettelheim in his discussion on the deviationist trends in socialist countries. In several works on socialist transition in the USSR and China, Bettelheim pointed out that whether the proletariat was exercising political power and class struggle was proceeding on all fronts to ensure socialist progress were important points. According to him the question of allowing market forces to operate, giving material incentives for work and autonomy to enterprises, have to be discussed within that framework.[6] In his analysis, however, Bettelheim did not pay adequate attention to the linkage of the political question with the objective problems in society. But we do find a key to the central question in Bettelheim's analysis, namely, that without the political perspective of the working people economic development may cause further alienation.

Therefore, the new political economy of socialist development has to comprehend the objective problems in socialist society in an integral perspective and stress the centrality of the political dimension. It is in this vein that we talk of socialism in the freedom scale. Arun Bose has given a timely call for 'radical rethinking in search for new starting points for communist-managed socialist societies at every level: technological, economic, political, and not least, philosophic.'[7]

These are issues which have been debated in the PRC and keeping them in mind one should evaluate China's development record.

China's Development Performance

China has an impressive record of progress since 1949. A backward economy which frequently experienced famine conditions and a war-ravaged society which fell victim to imperialist plunder has travelled quite a distance since liberation. There is some justification for the claim of the CPC General Secretary in his 40th anniversary speech when he says that China has been turned from a 'poor and blank' semi-

Table 1: Growth of National Income, Agricultural and Industrial Production of China (Average year-to-year per cent change)

	1953-78	*1979-88*	*1979-84*	*1985-88*	*1979-2009*	*1991-2009*
National income	6.0	9.3	8.3	10.7	9.9	10.5
National income per-capita	3.9	7.8	6.9	9.3	7.3(U)* 7.2(R)**	8.3(U) 5.5(R)
Agricultural output	2.9	6.2	7.7	3.9	6.0	6.0
Industrial production	11.3	12.8	9.6	17.8	–	–
Light industry	9.3	14.9	12.3	19.0	–	–
Heavy industry	13.8	10.9	7.2	16.6	–	–

Source: State Statistical Bureau, *Statistical Yearbook of China, 1988* and *China Statistical Yearbook, 2010*.
*U-Urban, **R-Rural

colonial and semi-feudal country into an 'initially prosperous socialist country'. The Chinese people have a degree of security and dignity of living and their country has acquired a respectable status in the world. Therefore, despite the cloud of the Tian'anmen episode the people of China have good reasons to celebrate their revolution's anniversary.

Improvement of material conditions in China has been the most conspicuous gain since 1949. As Tables 1, 2, and 3 show, there has been considerable growth of production in practically every sector. The gross national product in 1988 was 19.8 times that of 1949 and the national income 18 times. The actual

Table 2: Foodgrains Output in China (million metric-tons)

Year	*Output*	*Annual Change (Per cent)*
1951	143	—
1955	184	8.2
1960	158	10.7
1965	195	– 5.8
1970	247	9.3
1975	280	1.8
1976	286	2.1
1977	283	– 1.0
1978	304	7.4
1979	332	9.2
1980	321	– 3.3
1981	325	1.2
1982	353	8.6
1983	387	9.6
1984	407	5.2
1985	379	– 6.9
1986	391	3.2
1987	402	2.8
1988	394	– 2.0
2000*	462.1	–
2005*	484.0	–
2011*	571.21	4.5

Source: *Economic Growth in China and India: A Perspective by Comparison* by Subramaniam Swamy.
* *China Statistical Yearbook*, 2006, 2011.

consumption level of the people was 76 yuan in 1952 which has grown to 639 yuan in 1988. The average life-span of the Chinese people has increased from thirty-five years in pre-Liberation China to 73.5 years during 11th Five Year Plan (2006-10) period.

Table 3: Structure of China's GDP

(Per cent)

	1952-65	*1966-78*	*1979*	*1987*	*2010*
Agriculture	44.8	39.3	36.6	33.8	10.9
Industry	33.1	43.0	48.6	45.7	48.6
Services	22.1	17.7	14.8	20.4	40.5
of which					
Commerce	13.2	9.7	7.3	10.1	–
Transportation	4.5	3.8	3.6	3.7	–
Construction	4.4	4.2	3.9	6.6	–

Source: *Statistical Yearbook of China, 1988* and *China Statistical Yearbook, 2011.*

Table 4: China Since 1978 Reforms

	Gross Value of Output (index)		*Death Rate (index)*		*Female-male Ratio*
	Industry	*Agriculture*	*National*	*Rural*	*(value)*
1979	100	100	100	100	94.3
1980	109	104	102	101	94.4
1981	113	111	102	102	94.2
1982	122	123	106	110	94.1
1983	135	135	114	120	93.9
1984	154	159	108	105	93.7
1985	181	181	106	104	93.5
1986	197	201	108	105	93.6
2010*	–	–	–	–	95.2

Sources: Compiled by Jean Dreze and Amartya Sen, *Hunger and Public Action* (Oxford: Clarendon Press, 1990) from People's Republic of China, *Statistical Yearbook of China 1988* (in English) I987 (in Chinese).
* *China Statistical Yearbook, 2011.*

Industrialization is regarded as a key to development even though it has to be subjected to the other dimensions of the freedom scale. China's record in industrialization has been fairly laudable. Fixed assets are 85 times more than that in 1949 and the industrial output value in 1988 was 134, times more. The average annual industrial growth rate during the forty-year period has been 13.4 per cent.[8] China leads the world in the production of coal and also cloth, ranks fourth in steel and electricity and holds fifth position in crude oil. In high-tech industry China has made significant strides. It is visible in the fields of aeronautics, nuclear energy, biotechnology and precision instruments. The present regime puts great emphasis on building a developed scientific and technological infrastructure.

The performance of Chinese agriculture has not been as dramatic as that of industry. The record of the reforms decade, particularly the period 1979-84, has been exceedingly positive; but the forty-year profile can at best be described as modest. Swamy's analysis of the Chinese and Indian performance in agriculture for the pre-reform period does not put a high score for China.[9] China's foodgrain output has increased from 143 million metric tonnes in 1951 to the peak of 407 million metric tonnes in 1984, but the per capita output of grain has moved from 288 kgs in 1952 to only 397 kgs in 1984 and has come down somewhat during the next few years. Even then, with the expansion of rural industries and sideline production, rural income has grown significantly during the last decade. During the decade of reforms the per capita net income of the farm population had an average annual growth rate of 11.8 per cent which was far higher than the same for the urban people (6.5 per cent). During the 1978-85 period peasant incomes doubled as a result of higher procurement prices for grains, introduction of institutional changes and incentive-based production policy. (During the preceding two decades peasant incomes had apparently risen by 80 per cent). The urban residents got less than a 50 per cent raise in their income during 1978-85. Thus there began a trend of change in the terms of trade in favour of the peasants. This has perhaps narrowed the rural-urban gap in recent years. The visible improvement in the standard of living of the rural residents—new houses, TV sets, washing machines, motorcycles—testifies to this trend. On the other hand, urban reforms have not raised the income of the city dwellers to the same extent.'[10]

Despite this impressive record there are problems which are noticed in various sectors of the economy. Even more important are the political and cultural corollaries of economic development. Even though there has been a steady rise in the living standards of the people, the overall level is still low in world standards with per capita national income close to India's where the magnitude of poverty is still substantial. Of course, the level of disparity of income and assets in China is not as large as in India. But inequality remains a problem to be tackled. The reforms decade has generated income disparities and it has alarmed the policy-makers. The disparities in regions constitute another serious problem. The inland areas in the northwest as well as the south, particularly minority areas, are pockets of underdevelopment while prosperity is concentrated in the coastal region.

Disproportionate development in various sectors has been another bottleneck. Overemphasis on certain industries without back up in terms of raw material and energy, and sometimes without ensuring demand for it, has been a feature in China very often causing both waste and parasitism. Other problems include low returns to investment, irrational allocation of capital, inefficient management and lack of coordination at various levels of the economy. All these problems have been taken into consideration from time to time and policies have been debated.

Improvement in the standard of living, reduction of inequalities and creation of democratic conditions of participation in the process of political-economic development are the essential dimensions of socialist construction. While living conditions have improved they are still low. Many inequalities persist and some new ones have emerged, even though the gross inequalities of feudal and capitalist societies do not exist in China. On the third aspect, namely, democratic process, the socialist institutions have not been adequately developed. On the other hand, the Communist Party through its central leadership exercises state power on behalf of the people. Its ideology is the only check against the arbitrary use of power. Even though much of the gains of the revolution can be attributed to the CPC from time to time, it has been seen that the Party's ideological line may be erroneous and cause serious setbacks in the pursuit of socialist goals. That is why there is a need for a democratic process in the society that allows people to participate in the decision-making process and question wrong policies.

The nature and course of economic development, their objectives and ideological and political lines have been subjects of intense political struggle in China. Which strategy of development has led to China's successes? How do we explain the deviations and lapses in socialist construction? From the viewpoint of the freedom scale what are the elements of an integral perspective for China's progress towards socialism? These questions take us to a discussion of Mao Zedong's perspective and the Deng Xiaoping line.

Mao and Deng in the Freedom Scale

Handling the Ten Major Relationships in a balanced way and maintaining the class struggle perspective throughout the period of socialism constitute the Maoist perspective on socialist construction. The post-Mao leadership however takes the Great Leap Forward and the Cultural Revolution, especially their negative dimensions which manifested themselves in course of their operation, into account as the Maoist perspective without seeing Mao's political economy in totality.

Even though the problems were picked out at random, they did compose an integrated strategy in Mao's speech of April 1956 when he identified the following ten relationships: (a) between heavy industry on the one hand and light industry and agriculture on the other; (b) industry in coastal regions and in the interior; (c) economic construction and defence construction; (d) between the state, units of production and the producers; (e) between central and local authorities; (f) between Han nationality and minority nationalities; (g) between Party and the non-Party; (h) between revolution and counter-revolution; (i) between right and wrong (dealing with those who have committed mistakes); and (j) between China and other countries. In fact some of the economic and political problems which crystallized later were anticipated by Mao at that point. He had advocated a cautious line, but a firm one with clearly identified socialist objectives. In fact, during the Hua Guofeng interlude after the fall of the Gang of Four the ten major relationships document was actually proclaimed as the guiding perspective. But it was dropped after the 3rd Plenum of the 11th Central Committee.

The integrating link was provided at the start of the Cultural Revolution when class struggle was identified as the key to socialist construction. This prescription of Mao which was later denounced by the Deng ideologues as idealist and anarchist, preventing smooth production process and over-emphasizing-production relations and underemphasizing the forces of production, was a method of assuring the direction of development. That the proletarian perspective should guide all activities and that socialist politics should command economy and other sectors was an effort to maintain the integrality of the socialist process. It may be true that the Cultural Revolution degenerated into factional power struggles at various levels and the rate of growth of production declined in some sectors; but in that perspective growth per se is not central to socialist construction. Growth towards what can now be called 'socialist freedom' is the main objective.'[11]

The 3rd Plenum of the 11th Central Committee of the CPC inaugurated the reform line under the leadership of Deng Xiaoping. Now this perspective has been given the status of theory in the 40th anniversary speech of CPC General Secretary. Jiang Zemin who has said:

> Comrade Deng Xiaoping's theory of construction of socialism with Chinese characteristics is a scientific one and therefore has been acknowledged and accepted by millions upon millions of the Chinese people.... We must, in the entire primary stage of socialism, be resolute and unswerving in implementing the basic line formulated by the 13th National Congress of the Party, lead and unite the people of all nationalities of the country, take economic construction as the core of our work, uphold the four cardinal principles, persist in the reform and opening and through self-reliance and hard work struggle to build our country into a

prosperous, democratic and culturally advanced modern socialist country.

The above formulation is a careful combination of different aspects of the policies of the reforms decade, some of which have been neglected from time to time. For example, simultaneous stress on the four principles (adherence to the socialist road, Communist Party leadership, the people's democratic dictatorship and Marxism-Leninism and Mao Zedong Thought), though proclaimed by Deng in March 1979, have been stressed mainly during the last two years while handling the student movement. Similarly, the final objective no doubt has a composite integral character, but the crucial policy guideline that focuses on economic construction through reform and open door has pushed China in a deviant direction. Deng's strategic plan for China to double its GNP by 1990 and double it again by the year 2000 to achieve close to 1000 US dollars per capita income for the Chinese has been given top priority at every level in China. It is justified by reference to the primacy of the productive forces forgetting that this development should lead China towards the socialist goal. This is where Mao had stressed the need for creating socialist values.

The reforms have been conducted under the framework of what the 3rd Plenum of the 13th Central Committee has christened as 'Socialist Commodity Economy'. Under this strategy of expanded market operation multiple forms of ownership—individual, joint stock companies, joint state-private, joint Chinese and multinational, besides cooperative and collective and state ownership—have developed rapidly in China. In other words, there is a distinctly new strata of capitalists who have emerged as a result of the new policies. No doubt, quantitatively they are a small force and it is claimed that their total assets are not more than five per cent of the entire industrial assets. But as a social and political force they symbolize the trend of inequality and privilege in addition to their entrepreneurial capacity.

Dismantling the rural people's communes and introduction of the contract responsibility system have immediately resulted in increased incomes in the countryside. But rising disparities in the rural areas, imbalances in grain production and excessive expansion of rural industries which have now faced many serious problems are some of the negative results of rural reforms. Even more serious is the decline, in public action on essential health and nutrition aspects resulting in increase in the proportion of infant mortality, adverse effects on women reflected in the falling sex ratio and increase in the death rate in rural areas which Amartya Sen has spoken of (Table 4).

The attack on the student movement in the name of fighting 'bourgeois liberalization' was a tragic irony. Reforms generated a consumerist, competitive, money-making climate and open door promoted incitement for capitalistic goods and services. In other words, the environment which saw the student upsurge was the direct result of the reform policies. It provided the social basis for the protest. The new managerial strata, capitalists, foreign-linked professionals and the powerful party cadres characterize the present stratification in China. The corruption and privileges with which these strata are associated were the targets of the student movement. Their demand was for democratization to alleviate the causes which gave rise to this phenomenon.

Thus we return to the central political question of democratizing the socialist state. The phenomenon of state socialism and party-state has caused considerable alienation. A new perspective on political economy of socialism involves not only the development of the material conditions but must also expand the realm of democratic practice and cultural creativity that is at once rooted in the people's own traditions and that of humanity, in the pursuit of socialist freedom. That would be a further celebration of revolution by the Chinese people.

NOTES

1. Andrew Gamble, 'Marxist Political Economy' in R.J. Barry Jones (Ed.), *The Worlds of Political of Economy* (London: Pinter Publishers, 1988).
2. Manoranjan Mohanty, 'Changing Terms of Discourse', *Economic and Political Weekly,* vol. xxiv, no. 37. Also, Rajni Kothari, *Rethinking Development* (Delhi: Ajanta, 1988).

3. Arun Bose, *Marxian and Post-Marxian Political Economy* (Penguin, 1975), Ch. 14.
4. K.K. Das Gupta, *Marxism and Political Economy of Socialism* (New Delhi: Sterling, 1989), p. 398.
5. Janos Komai, *Contradictions and Dilemmas* (Boston: MIT Press, 1986), p. 137.
6. Charles Bettelheim and Paul M. Sweezy, *On the Transition to Socialism* (New York: Monthly Review Press, 1971). See also Bettelheim, 'Great Leap Backward', *Monthly Review*, vol. 30, nos. 3 and 4.
7. Arun Bose, 'Political Economy of European Socialist Systems', Review of K.K. Das Gupta, *Economic & Political Weekly*, vol. xxiv, no. 37, p. 2075.
8. *News from China Supplement*, vol. 1, no. 43 (October 4, 1989). Speech by Jiang Zemin at the rally on September 29, 1989.
9. Subramaniam Swamy, *Economic Growth in China and India: A Perspective by Comparison* (New Delhi: Vikas, 1989).
10. Carl Riskin, *China's Political Economy* (Oxford: Oxford University Press, 1987), pp. 352-6.
11. Manoranjan Mohanty, 'On Socialist Freedom: Students' Movement in China', *Economic and Political Weekly*, vol. xxiv, no. 24.

6

Marxism and the Chinese Practice

During the rectification movement in Yenan, Mao Zedong had repeatedly called for creative application of Marxist ideology to the concrete conditions of China. His purpose was to theorize on the strategic experience of the Chinese communist movement within the broad Marxist theory of revolution but without drawing parallels with the Bolshevik Revolution. The post-Mao leaders of China claim to have used the same methodology to advance their drive for modernization and to build what they call socialism with Chinese characteristics. Like Mao in the 1940s, Deng Xiaoping and his colleagues too insisted on taking ideology not as a dogma but as a guide to action. In fact they used quotations from Mao's 1937 essay "On Practice" to assert that only those principles which have stood the test of practice are valid. Integration of theory and practice is the common theme. But there are major differences between the two formulations. These differences have become conspicuous with the publication of Commentator's articles in *People's Daily* in December 1984.

The main difference lies in the fact that the Chinese leaders now identify certain ideas of Marx that have been historically invalidated. Incidentally, *People's Daily's* commentator has always been an authoritative spokesman of the CPC and therefore can be taken to be speaking for Deng's group today. The earlier practice with various communist parties of the world was to re-interpret specific formulations of Marx or to over-generalize them, i.e. giving them a broad meaning so as to obtain maximum flexibility for the current practitioner. That was Lenin's method of developing Marxism on questions of political economy of socialism, party organization or imperialism. In the same way Mao formulated the theory of 'new democratic revolution' without rejecting Marx's theory of bourgeois-democratic revolution. He developed the theory of class struggle in socialist society also by generalizing Marx's and Lenin's views on contradictions between the bourgeoisie and the proletariat.

Another difference between the experience of the Zhengfeng line of the 1940s and the present line is that the present leadership takes the experience of the developed capitalist countries to assess the backwardness of the socialist countries like China. In the earlier case the revolutionary experience of the CPC during the Sino-Japanese war was taken as the basis of the theoretical development of Marxism. Now the technological achievements of the West and its high levels of productivity are regarded as standards which the socialist countries as well should fulfil.

Thus the method of applying Marxist ideas to concrete revolutionary practice has itself undergone a change in recent years in China. That is where the significance of commentators' December articles lies. His article of December 7, 1984 entitled "Theory and Practice" was perhaps the boldest statement thus far on the inapplicability of certain ideas of Marx in the contemporary situation, and therefore it attracted world-wide attention. When questions were raised as to whether the CPC was abandoning Marxism, Commentator responded by publishing another article on December 21 explaining it further but reiterating the earlier position.

The process of ideological rectification in post-Mao China started with the Third Plenum of the Eleventh Central Committee in December 1978 where the Deng group won the political battle defeating the Hua Guofeng line. Thereafter a campaign "to emancipate thought" (*sixiang jiefang*) was launched mainly to encourage people to give up the ideas of Cultural Revolution. In that process two ideological trends emerged. Some wanted to denounce Mao Zedong Thought while others questioned the feasibility of Marxism itself. In 1978

Deng had given a call to take "practice as the sole criterion of truth", and to examine the validity of the ideological formulations of Mao Zedong.

During the next two years many people in China frankly advocated the adoption of liberal democracy. In 1980 Deng again intervened to steer the debate in a certain direction, and to set the line of assessment of Mao Zedong Thought. Deng said that Mao's major contribution to the victory of the revolution in China must be acknowledged, and on the whole due honour in history must be accorded to him by the Chinese people. But his mistakes in socialist construction both in terms of theory and in practice must be repudiated. In other words, Mao's ideas of Great Leap Forward and Cultural Revolution should be thoroughly criticized as manifesting his "leftist" and subjective deviation. Particularly, Mao's theory of class struggle in a socialist society came under heavy fire. Accordingly, the Eleventh Central Committee in its Sixth Plenum in June 1981 adopted the resolution on "Certain questions in the history of our Party" spelling out its evaluation of Mao and giving its view of the events of the post-1949 period.

The new economic policies, like the production responsibility system in agriculture, were put into extensive practice, the ideological debate took a new turn. When the liberal democratic elements persisted in their attack on Marxism, Party theoreticians came out defending the communist ideology. In 1982, for example, Politbureau member and the then President of the Chinese Academy of Social Sciences, Hu Qiaomu, came out with an article in *People's Daily* (September 24) entitled "On the Practice of Communist Thought", wherein he tried to meet the argument of the liberal critics. The critics had pointed out that since no communist society had yet come into being anywhere in the world, there was no basis for communist thought. He pointed out that the practice of the communist movement both before and after the revolution provided the basis for communist thought.

Thus the Chinese ideologues had to face criticism now from the right and now from the left. The present series of articles have appeared in response to the left critics. These articles further attack the remnants of what they regard as "leftist influence". Since a massive organizational purge started in the Party in 1983 it was possible that some critics were attacking the prevailing policies as being non-Marxist. These critics need not be defenders of the Cultural Revolution or even of Mao's economic ideas. They may have said that some of the new economic policies violated classical Marxist principles of political economy. "Yes, so what?" Deng and his theoretician colleagues might retort, "some of Marx's ideas have been proved incorrect".

The present-day leaders of China assert that Marx has been proved wrong on his theory that commodity exchange will disappear in the socialist system. To back up their argument they refer to Lenin's early experiment in restricting commodity exchange, and to his reversal of that line in 1921 to reintroduce elements of market economy. The Chinese leaders argue that commodity production must be encouraged in the socialist system in order to advance the productive forces. For this purpose there should be competition among producers and enterprises. The prices should be generally determined by the forces of demand and supply in the market. Individual and group initiative should be encouraged and performance rewarded. This is how the growth of the commodity economy would facilitate development of production.

On the basis of this theory the Deng Xiaoping group has disbanded the people's communes and allotted land to families on contract basis for cultivation. Private commerce has grown in the countryside as well as towns. Wages and bonuses are linked with workers' productivity. Workers compete with one another for producing more for more remuneration. Losing enterprises have to pay for their poor performance. Private investment in shops, factories and various other agencies has grown. Earnings may now be spent on buying modern gadgets, building houses, going abroad, etc. All these are instances of developing the commodity economy which is a characteristic of the capitalist system. The Chinese think that operation of the commodity economy is one of the economic laws which is valid both for capitalist and socialist economies.

What then makes it a socialist economy? The Chinese answer is threefold. Firstly, the state-run economy is the mainstay of the national economy, and thus the basic system of public ownership of the means of production does exist in China. Individual enterprise and other non-socialist economic forms are believed to be meant for making up the deficiencies in the socialist sector of the economy. Secondly, the socialist principle of "to each according to his work" has been implemented in China, whereas in a capitalist economy workers' wages are determined after the appropriation of the surplus value by the capitalists. This, of course, discards the Cultural Revolution notion of "eating from the iron bowl", i.e. equalitarian distribution irrespective of different levels of performances. The Chinese leaders claim that their wage system is neither adventurist nor capitalist. Thirdly, China's planned economy is guided by a socialist state led by the Communist Party and it ensures proportionate growth of different sectors of the economy and steady well-being of the working people.

However, the Chinese leaders' critique of Marx suffers from a fallacy. Marx has not elaborately discussed the political economy of socialism. What we find in Marx's writings is a detailed analysis of the capitalist economy with a brief discussion of communist principles. The difference between the lower and higher stages of communism is also mentioned briefly. The Chinese leaders assume that what Marx attributed to communism—the abolition of the commodity exchange—was true of the socialist or the lower phase. What Marx's writings suggest is that the socialist revolution entails the emergence of a new political economy where commodity exchange is gradually regulated and restricted, so that conditions are slowly created to move towards communism. The crucial difference between Marx's stipulation and Deng's is that while the former advocated the restriction of the market economy the latter supports its growth. Moreover, the present-day Chinese leaders do not regard these measures as temporary, like Lenin did, but assure again and again that these policies would continue for generations to come. Within the framework of "one country, two systems" (i.e. coexistence of socialist and capitalist forms) these policies are not taken as short-term adjustment measures. Chinese theorists of today find Marx's formulation on socialist political economy unacceptable because it does not support their present-day policies. It is unacceptable to them because they are committed to a set of growth-oriented policies on market lines. The Chinese leaders had the option of explaining these policies in terms of 'people's democracy' as in the early years of the Republic. But they seem to have decided to defend these policies as "socialism with Chinese characteristics".

In this sense it is a departure from the core principle of Marxist political economy of transition from capitalism to socialism. Creative development of Marxism is the norm of dialectical materialist notion of knowledge. But when a core principle is abandoned, it raises serious doubts about the Marxist credentials of the policies. The recent assertion in China therefore signals a trend of erosion of Marxism in China.

7

Power of History: Mao Zedong Thought and Deng's China

METHOD OF DISCRIMINATING EVALUATION

Successor generations have several options to define their relationship with the leaders of their social movements. One is to elevate the leader into a cult figure and ritually pay respect. In such cases, the values and goals of the leader are put on a high pedestal in an abstract form and commitment to them is reaffirmed by the new leaders. This probably has been the way Gandhi was treated by Nehru and his successors. Another way is to overgeneralize the ideas of a leader so as to generate a large spectrum of interpretations. Thus, besides maintaining a cult, the successors continue to affirm their adherence to the founder's principles: This is how Lenin was treated by the later Soviet leaders and many communists in different parts of the world. A third mode is to sharply break with the earlier leader and after denouncing the predecessor announce a new line. Khrushchev's denunciation of Stalin falls in this category.

Deng Xiaoping's assessment of Mao Zedong did not adopt any of the three approaches. He followed what can be called the method of discriminating evaluation—a method that Mao applied to analyse Stalin's role and his ideas. This method identifies the criteria of judgement, particularly the vantage point of the observer and after having a total view of a leader, proceeds to find the positive and negative aspects of the leader's role and ideas. The total view presents the summary perspective as to whether the leader ought to be on the whole admired or condemned. Accordingly, the positive aspects would be primary or secondary. This is how Mao assessed Stalin to be '70 per cent right and 30 per wrong.'[1] Similarly Deng Xiaoping has stated that Mao's 'contributions were primary and his mistakes were secondary.'[2] In some cases the mistakes of the great leaders are either not discussed at all or explained away in terms of contingencies of the prevailing situation. Analysing Gandhi's mistakes is a taboo in many quarters in India as is critical scrutiny of Sun Yatsen's role in China. The popular adoration of such national figures is so widespread that discriminating evaluation becomes difficult except as deliberate exercises.

In the application of this method, the vantage point of assessment is critical. Mao viewed Stalin both when the latter was alive and after his death, from the standpoint of the leader of the Chinese revolution and socialist construction. Mao was engaged in finding a Chinese path for a democratic and a socialist revolution and that influenced his judgement on Stalin. Even though Stalin's directives to the CPC in the 1920s and 30s caused considerable harm to the communist movement and several of Stalin's policies in the 40s and the early 50s offended China's nationalist sentiments, still Mao paid homage to Stalin for his leadership of the USSR during the Second World War. Mao actually traced Soviet revisionism to Stalin's 'walking on one leg' or one-sided policies and violation of democratic centralism. While proposing the 'mass line' as the alternative to Stalin's bureaucratic centralization and political terror, Mao however, refused to totally denounce Stalin.[3] Whether the later events exposing the fragility of the Soviet state and its collapse would warrant a further evaluation of Stalin is another important question.

Deng Xiaoping's vantage point was China's economic construction. The context was the passing away of Zhou Enlai, Zhu De and Mao in quick succession in 1976, the arrest of the Gang of Four and the formal termination of the Cultural Revolution. A cult of Mao had been built up during the period of the Cultural Revolution (CR). In the two years following the fall of the Gang of Four when Hua Guofeng was the CPC

Chairman and Premier there was an intense debate on various ideological and political issues in China. Hua's line of defending the basic orientation of the CR while pushing for a strategy of four modernizations was finally defeated and Deng's line of 'reform and open door' achieved victory at the Third Plenum of the Eleventh Central Committee in December 1978. After that Deng and his colleagues decided to orient every policy to serve the needs of economic development.

The official denunciation of the CR was so strong and it seemed to have so much public support that it could have engulfed a total condemnation of Mao Zedong. In fact, many posters on the Democracy Wall in February-March 1979 called for de-Maoization like Khrushchev's de-Stalinization in Russia. Many leaders who had been harassed by Mao–including Deng Xiaoping and Chen Yun–could have taken that line. But Deng himself took the initiative to stem that tendency and called for a careful assessment of Mao Zedong and Mao Zedong Thought. The CPC Central Committee appointed a group headed by General Secretary Hu Yaobang in 1980 to formulate a document on this question. After much deliberations and many revisions in which Deng himself participated in the Resolution on Certain Questions in the History of Our Party was adopted at the Sixth Plenum in June 1981. The 1981 Resolution spelt out the perspective of discriminating evaluation relating to Mao which guided the public discussion on Mao during the reform period right up to the celebrations of the Mao Zedong Birth Centenary on December 26, 1993.

Upholding and Developing

When one of the drafts of the Resolution on Party History was brought before Deng Xiaoping in 1980 he was upset by the fact that Mao Zedong's contribution to the Chinese revolution had not been adequately acknowledged. He said: 'If we don't mention Mao Zedong Thought and don't make an appropriate evaluation of Comrade Mao's merits and demerits, the old workers will not feel satisfied, nor will the poor and lower-middle peasants of the period of land reform, nor the many cadres who have close ties with them.'[4] This frank admission of the social basis of Mao's legacy was significant in itself. At the same time Deng knew the tremendous political advantages of maintaining a linkage between his reforms drive with Mao's historical role.

The most important linkage was the continuity of Chinese nationalism. Mao's declaration on the occasion of the proclamation of the PRC on October 1, 1949 was: 'Chinese people have stood up'. Deng's 1980 call to double China's GNP in ten years and quadruple it by the year 2000 so as to build a strong, prosperous modern and socialist China also had an electrifying effect. The themes of nationalism, modernization and democracy have dominated Chinese intellectual discourse for a century since the reforms debate of the 1990s. How to unite China, liberate it from colonial domination, build a strong and prosperous country to cope with Western challenges and eradicate poverty have been the common threads connecting Sun Yatsen, Mao Zedong and Deng Xiaoping and their respective generations of leaders. These goals and the movements for realizing them created widespread popular support for their organizations. Hence, the fund of legitimacy that was associated with the name of Mao Zedong could not be thrown away. Deng mobilized the party to affirm the contributions of Mao, but at the same time launched an altogether new line for socialist construction.

What would have appeared to be a delicate task, Deng made unambiguously sharp. His method consisted of (a) distinction between Mao Zedong and Mao Zedong Thought, (b) defining the essence of Mao Zedong Thought as seeking truth from facts, and (c) affirming Mao's contributions and criticizing Mao's mistakes, and selectively stressing specific principles from Mao Zedong Thought. It was such a composite approach that the present generation of leadership could 'uphold', i.e. adhere to and at the same time 'develop', i.e. alter in the light of changed circumstances the principles advocated by Mao Zedong. This was methodologically comparable to what Mao did to Marxism-Leninism by 'creatively applying it to the concrete conditions of China.' This is how the legacy of Mao was related to the reform programme under Deng's leadership. For this purpose a clear criticism was also made of Mao's policies during his last years, particularly relating to the Great Leap Forward (1958-60) and the Cultural Revolution (1966-76). How Deng himself took the lead in evolving a 'correct appraisal' of Mao Zedong was acknowledged by CPC General Secretary Jiang Zemin in his speech on the occasion of the Mao centenary at the Great Hall of the People in Beijing.

Mao and Mao Zedong Thought

A crucial distinction was made by Deng between Mao Zedong, the individual leader, and the system of ideas associated with his name. Almost as the distinction between Marx and Marxism, this exercise allows a continuous development of the ideological system with contributions from later leaders and movements. In fact, Deng Xiaoping's theory of building socialism with Chinese characteristics was acclaimed in 1992 as the latest component of Mao Zedong Thought.

The Seventh Congress of the CPC in April-June 1945 had for the first time adopted the Thought of Mao Zedong as part of its ideology along with Marxism-Leninism.' The Party Constitution defined the Thought of Mao as 'The integration of the Theory of Marxism-Leninism with the practice of the Chinese Revolution'. However, at the First Session of the Eighth Party Congress in 1956 the reference to Mao's ideas was removed from the CPC Constitution. During the CR, however, the leader and his Thought were merged and placed on a high pedestal. The Ninth Congress Constitution of the CPC referred to Mao Zedong Thought as the 'Marxism of the era in which imperialism was heading towards total collapse and socialism was advancing towards worldwide victory.'

That Deng was opposed to such a cult-building is evident from one of his speeches of 1960.[5] He strongly criticized vulgarization of Mao Zedong Thought by attributing heroic deeds in day-to-day life to it. Second, he asserted that Mao Zedong Thought should not be separated from Marxism-Leninism. Third, Mao Zedong was part of a collective leadership and its leader.

This approach was further articulated by Deng during

1978-80 in the course of the transition to the new framework. To begin with, there was a campaign against 'two whateverisms'. This aphorism referred to the claims by Hua Guofeng's supporters that the 'principles' laid down by Chairman Mao should be adhered to and 'instructions' on specific matters be carried out. Since Mao had personally appointed Hua as his successor, these claims had tremendous political implications. Deng advocated a complete break with the theory, ideology and policies of the CR and any effort to defend those had to be opposed. Hence a campaign to 'emancipate the mind' (*jiefang sixiang*) was launched to free the party cadres from being guided by the policies of the CR. As a consequence Hua was also criticized for his 'leftist' views and was replaced by Hu Yaobang in 1980.

While distinguishing Mao the leader from Mao Zedong Thought, Deng stressed the fact that there were many other leaders such as Zhou Enlai, Zhu De and Liu Shaoqi whose contributions should also be emphasized. The CR campaign against Liu had been denounced and his honour was restored by a special decision of the party in 1979. But within the collective, Mao Zedong was the most prominent leader. As Jiang Zemin put it in the Centenary speech, ... 'it was the first generation of the Party's central collective leadership with Comrade Mao Zedong at its core, that made pioneering and indelible contributions to building a new and modern socialist China.'

Mao's contribution is recognized in terms of his 'integration of the basic principles of Marxism-Leninism with China's reality'. The effort to seek a Chinese path to revolution in conditions of semi-colonialism and semi-feudalism was Mao's historical contribution.[6] He formulated the theory and strategy of new democratic revolution and evolved a series of policies and tactics to carry forward the liberation struggle. Jiang has listed them: 'He opened up a revolutionary road of building rural revolutionary base areas, encircling the cities from rural areas and seizing political power with armed force.' It is interesting to note that in his 'Long Live the Victory of People's War' celebrating the twentieth anniversary of the victory over Japan in 1965, Lin Biao too had summed up Mao's contribution in similar terms. Jiang Zemin described Mao as 'a great Marxist, a proletarian revolutionary, a military strategist and a theoretician, ... a great patriot and a national hero in contemporary China.'

Acknowledging the influence that Mao's ideas had had outside China, Jiang said: 'Comrade Mao Zedong, as a great historical figure not only belongs to China, but also to the world.' This is important because the same was not claimed for Deng Xiaoping's ideas. Deng's theory of building socialism was christened with particular reference to China rather than being generalized for comparable parts of the world.

As distinct from the leader or person Mao Zedong, Mao Zedong Thought has been understood by the Deng leadership as the collective wisdom of the party. As Jiang Zemin put it: 'CPC members, with Comrade Mao Zedong as their chief representative, theoretically summed up China's experiences ... in accordance with the basic tenets of Marxism-Leninism, moulding them into a scientific guiding ideology suited to China's conditions.' Describing it as 'a complete, scientific ideological system' with 'original theories on a wide range of ideas', Jiang identified three basic aspects of Mao Zedong Thought as 'seeking truth from facts, the mass line and maintaining independence and keeping the initiative in one's own hands'.

This formulation linked Mao's ideas with Marxist tradition and at the same time emphasized the principles emerging from Chinese revolutionary experiences. Mao's role in this process is acknowledged, but other Chinese leaders also contributed to the 'theoretical treasure house' of the CPC. It is a body of crystallized principles, but it is always subject to further enrichment. Thus, the distinction between Mao and Mao Zedong Thought became an important political device to proceed on a new road of development with the reforms package after 1978 while paying homage to Mao Zedong at the same time.

In fact, 'the one focus and two points' framework of Deng's modernization programme had 'Marxism-Leninism-Mao Zedong Thought' which Deng proclaimed in March 1979 as one of the Four Cardinal Principles. (Economic construction is the focus. One point is reform and open door. The other point is adherence to the four cardinal principles—socialist road, People's Democratic Dictatorship, Leadership of the CPC and Marxism-Leninism-Mao Zedong Thought. In 1979 Deng had spoken of the Dictatorship of the Proletariat which was reformulated later.)

Seeking Truth From Facts

The theoretical device which Deng adopted for purposes of relating Mao's legacy with his reforms programme was the doctrine of 'seeking truth from facts'. This essentially meant accepting those principles which delivered results in practice and rejecting those which did not work. What is more, this doctrine, Deng asserted, was the essence of Mao Zedong Thought. Thus, Deng derived a method and legitimacy from Mao to unfurl a new path of development.

Mao had inscribed *shishi qiushi* (seek truth from facts) while laying the foundation for the party school at Yan'an in 1942. That was the period when Mao was attacking dogmatic interpretations of Marxism and Leninism, especially the Russian path of revolution. Earlier, in 1930 he had attacked 'book worship'.

In 1940 he had articulated the ideology and strategy of the Chinese revolution in his essay *On New Democracy*. It had become clear that the CPC under his leadership had found its own path to fight colonialism and feudalism and unite China after going through a process of trial and error. Through political practice the CPC had tested various ideas and had arrived at the 'correct knowledge'.

This method had been dealt with by Mao in his 1937 essay *On Practice*. One begins with existing concepts and ideas and in course of practice they are tested, confirmed or disproved. Again, those ideas are put to practice. A long process of such exercises leads to rational knowledge. There is, however, no end to this process of interaction between knowledge and practice. Knowledge is constantly refined and enriched through practice.[7] As the 1981 Resolution on CPC History stated, '... truth is inexhaustible and that truth of any piece of knowledge, namely, whether it corresponds to objective reality, can ultimately be decided only through social practice.'[8]

Using this philosophical weapon, Deng launched a drive in 1979 for 'taking practice as the sole criterion of truth'. After all Mao himself had pursued this line while evolving a new path of revolution in China. So his successors were called upon to apply the same method to Mao's policies, specially of the preceding decade. This political strategy was used to accomplish a sharp break with the Cultural Revolution and eliminate the influence of even moderate leaders of the transitional period such as Hua Guofeng.

'Seeking truth from facts' or testing knowledge through constant practice makes every idea dynamic and developmental and gives a pragmatic outlook to policy making. It is an extremely useful notion that every leader would like to propagate. But there is a complex dimension of this principle which may reduce it to a crude utilitarian doctrine. What is the span of experience in time and place which decides the validity of a principle? What is the procedure for aggregating the experiences and evaluating a principle? Are not alternative judgements possible for the same set of empirical evidence if vantage points and criteria are different?[9] In fact, the debate on Deng's reform policies has precisely raised these questions. But undoubtedly, this formulation served a serious political purpose of Deng for openly pointing out Mao Zedong's mistakes and proposing an alternative path of modernization of China.

Mao's Mistakes

The 1981 Resolution on CPC History traces Mao's mistakes to the launching of the Greap Leap Forward in 1958. Prior to that besides acknowledging Mao's theory of new democratic revolution and a series of policies and principles which consolidated the newly established People's Republic, it underlined the significance of two of Mao's works, *On Ten Great Relations* (1956) and *On the Correct Handling of Contradictions Among People* (1957). The first article stressed the need for balanced development of various sectors of the economy and society. The second sought to unite maximum social forces or 'people', i.e. apart from the small number of enemy forces, to build socialism. For the current programme of socialist modernization Deng advocated a similar scale of united efforts of popular forces including the national bourgeoisie.

According to Deng's assessment, Mao erred when he tried to reverse the programme of the Eighth Congress of the CPC of 1956. That Congress had announced the establishment of a socialist system and had declared that the principal contradiction now was between productive forces which were still backward and people's material needs. But Mao took the view that the principal contradiction was between the working class and the bourgeoisie. In other words, while the former view implied a focus on economic construction, the latter led to continuing class struggle through political mobilization. That divide persisted for the next two decades and Mao launched the Cultural Revolution to emphasize the politics of class struggle. After Mao's death and the fall of the Gang of Four, Deng essentially mobilized those members of the Eighth Central Committee and Politbureau who had been persecuted in course of the Cultural Revolution and launched the drive for four modernizations.

The two errors of Mao that the 1981 Resolution highlighted were the error of 'broadening the scope of class struggle' and 'undermining the principle of collective leadership'.[10] The former led to the 'catastrophe of the Cultural Revolution' creating anarchy in Chinese society and disrupting production. It also violated, according to Deng, the basic principle of historical materialism which stressed the primacy of material or productive forces. The latter led to the building up of a Mao cult which violated the principle of inner party democracy. As the coup attempt of Lin Biao and manoeuvres of the Gang of Four proved, this situation was taken advantage of by several factional leaders to settle scores with their opponents.

The 1981 Resolution decrees thus: 'Chief responsibility for the grave left error of the "Cultural Revolution", an error comprehensive in magnitude and protracted in duration, does indeed lie with Comrade Mao Zedong. But it was the error of a great proletarian revolutionary.'[11]

Despite this sharp critique much care was taken to point out as to how Mao protected many cadres during the CR, rehabilitated several senior leaders, criticized Jiang Qing and some other leaders and frustrated their designs and kept administration and the economy going during the decade of the Cultural Revolution. The Resolution stated: '... if we judge his activities as a whole, his contributions to the Chinese revolution far outweigh his mistakes. His merits are primary and his errors secondary.'[12] The same sentiments were echoed by Jiang Zemin in his centenary address as well.

Once the Deng leadership worked out a method of inheriting Mao's legacy and at the same time repudiating his model of socialist construction it was easy to proceed with the new economic policies of 'reform and open door'. On specific occasions Mao's formulations were invoked selectively. On inviting foreign capital, for example, the principle of 'maintaining initiative and independence' was cited in defence of national dignity. To curb the spread of values such as greed, selfishness and money-making, Mao's writings 'Serve the People', 'Learn from Lei Feng' were recalled. To check bureaucratism in the party and government, references were made to Mao's stress on the mass line. In other words, this framework allowed empirical utilization of Mao's ideas on particular problems, despite the clear rebuttal of Mao's theory and policies on class struggle in socialist society.

This perspective served the reform process spanning fifteen years rather well. But every time there was a crisis, Mao's alternative perspective inevitably formed part of the discourse. For example, there were some elements among the wide spectrum of forces of youth and students in Tian'anmen Square in April-June 1989 who recalled Mao's participatory socialism.[13] But on the whole, the economic success of the reforms and China's rising status in the world provided a degree of vindication to Deng's approach to Mao. Yet the politics of the centenary celebrations brought forth some interesting questions.

Politics of Centenary

The preparations for the celebrations of the birth centenary of

Mao Zedong clearly indicated that Mao Zedong Thought had become an object of political and ideological struggle in China. Mao's legacy had itself become a political force; therefore, the Chinese leaders had to evolve ways of coping with the power of history. The nature and scale of the celebrations had to be oriented in the right direction lest they had adverse effects on the course of Deng's reforms.

As the centenary approached there was a sudden upsurge in the appearance of mementoes on Mao in 1992. Buttons, posters, sketches and artefacts flooded the streets all over China. Songs of the 1950s and 60s including the ones which were most popular during the Cultural Revolution such as 'East in Red' and 'Ode to the Helmsman' were re-recorded by prominent singers of modern China. Audio and video cassettes were sold in millions. The 'Karaoke' (dance halls) in most restaurants played Mao songs with film clips from the earlier years to the tune of which men and women danced. By early 1993, the onset of the centenary year, the popular wave of paying homage to Mao Zedong was so widespread that there were reactions in several quarters.

Messages were sent to the CPC leaders that some people may use the occasion of the centenary to revive 'ultra-left' ideas. So the party was advised to take precautionary measures to ensure that the reforms were not derailed. Already in the wake of the Tian'anmen uprising, after the collapse of the Soviet Union, some leaders had tried to slow down the process of marketization and opening to foreign capital during 1990-91. Deng's visit to Shenzhen and other Special Economic Zones in January-February 1992 reversed that trend and resumed the pace of development. In April 1993 there was reportedly a meeting of the party leaders including Deng Xiaoping, Peng Zhen and Wan Li where it was decided that the Mao birth centenary celebrations should be 'moderate and not excessive'.[14]

Pressures exerted on the party to monitor the scale of celebrations included those from the All China Federation of Industry and Commerce (ACFIC). In a letter to the CPC Central Committee in August 1993 the ACFIC opposed the tendency to 'revive the Mao cult' pointing out that it might seriously undermine the confidence of non-party personnel and industrialists in the programme of four modernizations. Around the same time thirty-two writers including the famous novelist Ba Jin and historian Zhou Gucheng signed a petition calling for a halt to the building of the Mao cult.[15]

One of the indications of the low key official stance was the absence of a national committee for the centenary celebrations with representations from the party, state and army. In order to avoid hurting the sensitivity of the non-communist forces, there was an attempt to project some of the main activities as party level activities. Three departments of the party, namely, the Propaganda Department, the Institute of Party Literature and Department of Party Archives; the General Political Department of the PLA and the State Education Commission—these five bodies were responsible for the celebrations at the national level.[16] A controversy arose as to whether Bo Yibo's book, *A Review of Several Major Policy Decisions and Events* (Vol. II) covering the period of the Great Leap Forward should be recommended to party cadres. Apparently it did not sufficiently criticize Mao for his mistakes. The party school believed that whereas the book should be available to the public it need not be part of the curriculum in party study circles.[17]

Eventually the scale of celebrations did not appear small at all. Numerous bodies, universities, institutes and associations in various provinces and cities had their own programmes. In Shaoshan, Mao's birth place in Hunan, a new copper statue of Mao was installed and a museum was inaugurated. Mao's poems were engraved on stone.

Memorial meetings were held all over China with a great deal of fanfare. Hundreds of new publications appeared in the market. A new multi-volume anthology of Mao's works containing many items unpublished so far was brought out by the Central Institute of Party Literature. A collection of Mao's writings on military affairs and another on diplomatic work were also published on this occasion. A new detailed chronicle of Mao's life, a picture album of reminiscences on Mao by veteran revolutionaries were some of the other highlights. Films on Mao attracted full houses in China and were screened by

Chinese missions abroad. Finally, the centenary meeting at the Great Hall of the People on December 23, 1993 which was televised live gave a grand finale to the centenary celebrations. CPC General Secretary Jiang Zemin spoke on the occasion and Premier Li Peng presided over the meeting.

Power of History

Politics of the centenary celebrations acknowledged the power of history and brought to the surface the fact that the legacy of Mao Zedong had become an integral part of popular consciousness in China. The party leadership had to orient this consciousness towards the reforms programme. This was done by the party's theoreticians working hard to piece together a theory on the reforms which could perhaps match Mao's contributions. This came in the form of Deng Xiaoping's theory of building socialism with Chinese characteristics.

In October 1992 at the Fourteenth Congress of the CPC the concept of 'socialist market economy' was spelt out and so was Deng's theory. Originally, however, Deng's theory was announced by Jiang Zemin in his speech celebrating the 40th anniversary of the foundation of the PRC in 1989. The 'socialist market economy' entailed treating the 'market', 'management' and 'technology' as instruments of transition from a traditional economy to a modern economy rather than features of capitalism. And China was developing its productive forces by using these instruments. Thus, the concept of the 'primary stage of socialism' which was articulated at the Thirteenth Party Congress in 1987 was further developed through this exercise. On the foundation of these premises Deng was credited to have formulated his 'theory of building socialism with Chinese characteristics'. It was argued that not having gone through a process of capitalist industrialization, China had an underdeveloped level of productive forces. Hence China had to pursue a comprehensive programme of economic development with the help of capital and technology from all over the world. It also involved using multiple forms of ownership, public and private, and pursuing a distribution system based on production responsibility (i.e. wage determined by profit and losses). Through the maintenance of macro-economic control and Communist Party leadership this path of development was to be pursued. Combining planning and market, public and private ownership and maintaining political control by the CPC and interacting with the world economy are some of the Chinese characteristics in course of socialist construction in contemporary China. This is how the 'one focus and two points' framework mentioned earlier was put in the form of a theory.

Referring to Deng's theory, Jiang Zemin said in his centenary speech: 'This epitomizes another new historical leap for our Party of integrating Marxism with the realities of China.' Calling it 'the Marxism of contemporary China', Jiang described it as 'an unprecedented brand new creation in the history of the development of socialism.' Deng was described to have 'inherited and developed Mao Zedong Thought'. Jiang said: 'He (Deng) proves himself to be Comrade Mao Zedong's loyal comrade-in-arms, as well as a most prominent heir to and developer of Mao Zedong Thought.'[18]

It may be recalled that the personal treatment that Mao meted out to Deng was in the extremes. In 1957 Mao reportedly told Khrushchev in Moscow that Deng was the brightest (*zui congming*) among his colleagues. But Deng was twice dismissed from his post during the Cultural Revolution. Mao and Zhou Enlai had restored Deng to take charge of the Central Committee in 1973-4. All that was part of history.

The process of building up the political and theoretical image of Deng was heightened during 1992-3 in China. Deng's 'statements in his southern tour' in early 1992 became the stimulus and reference point for cadres and managers of enterprises to speed up production with great enthusiasm. Many cadres believed that the best way to avert a Soviet-type of collapse in China was to achieve economic development, satisfy the material demands of people and maintain stability under party control. Economic successes, therefore, provided the basis for Deng's popularity among the Chinese people. The release of the third volume of Deng's *Selected Works* was marked by a campaign to study Deng's Theory.[19] The party propagated the view that just as Mao had contributed an innovative path of revolution, Deng presented an innovative path of socialist development.

History, however, is a difficult terrain full of tough tests. Deng's definition of socialism represents one model of society while Mao's another. For Deng, 'the essence of socialism is to emancipate and develop productive forces, eliminate exploitation and polarization and finally realize common prosperity.[20] This is no doubt a grand enough vision to excite the imagination of people to build a new society. No doubt, economic growth in China, rising prosperity of the Chinese people and China's prestige in the world have vindicated the success of Deng's strategy. But increasing social and regional disparities, corruption, crimes and decadent cultural practices have caused widespread anxiety in China. The Mao birth centenary provided an occasion to evaluate the reforms. The contemporary modernizers had to place their programme against the history of the Chinese revolution. For Mao, there was something more in the agenda for socialism in addition to economic development—the creation of a socialist human being with a moral-political consciousness. The achievement of this was historicized, in a long but defined period for a stage-by-stage movement towards the goals of equality and freedom progressively distinguishing such a society from the alienated and atomized capitalist society. Even newer questions have emerged from the aftermath of the collapse of Soviet Union. Was it essentially an economic failure? Or did it move farther and farther from the socialist vision? Deng may have found economic and political answers to some of these questions. Mao had raised some questions earlier through his stress on class struggle. Perhaps history would demand further creative responses in future to the growing urges of socialist freedom.[21]

NOTES

1. Manoranjan Mohanty, 'Mao's Portrait of Stalin'. *China Report*, vol. xi, no. 4, July-August 1975, Chapter 2 in this volume.
2. Deng Xiaoping, 'Uphold Mao Zedong Thought', *Selected Works of Deng Xiaoping (1975-1982).*

3. 'On the Historical Experiences of Dictatorship of the Proletariat', *The People's Daily*, Editorial, April 5, 1956 which dealt with this question is generally attributed to Mao. On the same theme, also see the one on December 29, 1956.
4. Deng Xiaoping, op. cit., 'Remarks on Drafts on CPC History', p. 284.
5. Deng Xiaoping, 'Correctly Disseminate Mao Zedong Thought' (March 25, 1960), in *Selected Works of Deng Xiaoping (1938-1965)* (Beijing: Foreign Languages Press, 1992).
6. Manoranjan Mohanty, *The Political Philosophy of Mao Zedong* (New Delhi: Macmillan, 1978, 2nd ed. Delhi: Aakar Books, 2012).
7. Mao Zedong, 'On Practice', in *Four Essays on Philosophy* (Beijing: Foreign Languages Press, 1968). See also the chapter on 'Four Laws of Materialist Dialectics', in M. Mohanty, *The Political Philosophy of Mao Zedong*, op. cit.
8. *Resolution on CPC History* (*1949-81*) (Beijing: Foreign Languages Press, 1981), p. 68.
9. For a discussion of these issues see M. Mohanty, 'Between Truth and Revolution', *China Report*, vol. xvii, No. 1, January-February 1981.
10. *Resolution on CPC History*, op. cit., pp. 440-7.
11. Ibid., p. 41.
12. Ibid., p. 56.
13. M. Mohanty, 'For Socialist Freedom', *Economic and Political Weekly*, June 16, 1989.
14. *Daily Report: Foreign Broadcasting Information Service* (*FBIS*): China-93-198 , October 15, 1993, p. 22.
15. *Daily Report*: *FBIS*: China, October 6, 1993, pp. 24-5.
16. Some of this information is based on the author's discussions at the Institute of Marxism-Leninism Mao Zedong Thought at the Chinese Academy of Social Sciences in Beijing in August 1993.
17. *Daily Report*: *FBIS*: China, September 9, 1993, quoting Cheng Ming.
18. Jiang Zemin's speech, *Daily Report*: *FBIS*: China, December 29, 1993, pp. G7-8.
19. Apparently Deng himself disallowed the use of the term 'thought' (*sixiang*) for his ideas and approved the term 'theory' (*lilun*). It may be recalled that Mao had preferred *sixiang* to *zhuyi* (ism). This construction is based on the author's discussions at the Shanghai Academy of Social Sciences in August 1993.
20. Jiang's speech, op. cit., p. G5.
21. Manoranjan Mohanty, 'Mao, Deng and Beyond: Dialectics of Early Stage of Socialism', *China Report*, Special Number on 'New Course in China', vol. xx, Nos. 4 and 5, July-October 1984.

8

The New Ideological Banner: Deng Xiaoping Theory

THEORETICAL STATEMENT

A theoretical perspective of the reforms in post-Mao China has finally crystallized. Even though the fourteenth Party Congress of the CPC in 1992 had proclaimed 'Deng Xiaoping's Theory of Building Socialism with Chinese Characteristics', it was the fifteenth Congress which spelt it out in detail, located it in the history of Marxism and institutionalized it by making it part of the guiding ideology stated in the CPC Constitution. One of Deng's formulations was the concept of Primary Stage of Socialism which has also been proclaimed as the theoretical framework governing policies for the next century.

POLITICAL FUNCTIONS OF IDEOLOGY

Like all ideological exercises of the scale performed by the fifteenth Congress, this decision, too, sought to accomplish three tasks.

1. The adoption of Deng Xiaoping's Theory, firmly put forth *an enabling framework* of policies which Jiang Zemin can carry forward and can also innovate in changed conditions. The central principle of Deng's Theory expressly taken over from Mao but used for a different purpose, is 'seeking truth from facts' which permits the leaders to 'learn as you go on' and adjust one's

perspective to new situations.

2. It contributes to the process of *political consolidation* of the Jiang Zemin leadership, thus sidelining all those who oppose the 'banner' of Deng's Theory or those who differ with Jiang. Not being a charismatic leader like Mao or Deng, Jiang needs the 'banner' to protect his core position.
3. It allows *rationalization of power and policy*. Deng's Theory is described as being responsible for China's steady economic growth, its rising international status and improvement in the people's standard of living. With that banner up, the prevailing leadership can pursue policies that it thinks fit and can also defend its power and defend purges, shifts, or retirements of Jiang's critics in the party.

Thus, when Jiang called Deng's Theory the 'soul of the current Congress' he was using ideology to consolidate his power and rationalize his decisions.

Theory, Line and Banner

When Mao Zedong struck off *ism* (*zhuyi*) from the draft of a document and modestly approved of *thought* (*sixiang*) as the term for his guiding ideology of the CPC, what got enshrined in the Party Constitution was *Marxism-Leninism-Mao Zedong Thought*. The fifteenth Congress has added Deng's Theory of Building Socialism with Chinese Characteristics to the earlier formulation. The suffix *ism* is reserved for the founder philosopher Marx and the leader of the world's first socialist revolution. But the term 'theory' (*lilun*) does not reduce its centrality in contemporary China. Just as Mao Zedong Thought was the Marxism of his times, Deng's Theory is regarded as the Marxism of present-day China. In other words, everyone is asked to interpret Marx, Lenin and Mao the way Deng Xiaoping did. No doubt, Deng's stress on testing every idea with reference to facts or practice apparently allows alternative assessments but these assessments of past policies have been already made and summed up by Deng. Many other issues such as forms of ownership, role of the market, mode of distribution, pattern of enterprise management, use of technology, exercise of state power among others have also been settled and Deng's Theory is the epitome of these approaches. Thus, a fairly comprehensive system of ideas is embodied in Deng's Theory. So, but for the political decision by perhaps Deng himself, it could qualify for the higher status of an *ism* and as was also possible in the case of Mao.

Since the Third Plenum of the Eleventh Central Committee, the CPC has talked about the new *line* (*luxian*) and policies, though it has refrained from using the expression 'two line struggle' which was at the core of the Cultural Revolution (CR) discourse. Deng's new line started as a critique of the class struggle perspective of the CR. The first few years decided mainly on the new focus on economic development. This focus has continued to be the central theme in the reform period as well as the core of Deng's Theory. This focus was put forward as a programme of 'Reform and Open Door'–reform meaning changes in ownership forms, management practices, attitude to the market and distribution systems and open door meaning opening China to foreign capital and technology.

'Reform and Open Door' was considered good enough as the perspective for China's four modernization programmes. As a political safeguard to put the reforms under the CPC leadership, Deng formulated the Four Cardinal Principles in February 1979 which he invoked every time he had to cope with political disturbances. Since then, 'one central focus and two points' constituted the ideological line or the basic line of the party.

At the Thirteenth Congress in 1987 some of these policies were explained in terms of a formulation on the Primary Stage of Socialism. It was argued that since China had not gone through a capitalist phase, the forces of production had remained backward; hence there was a need for a long period of the primary stage when production could develop emulating even some capitalist experiences in the fields of advanced technology and market practices. But this notion was not used consistently during the intervening period. The Fifteenth Congress has affirmed it as a part of Deng's Theory and Jiang

Zemin has explained it in detail in a separate section devoted to the Primary Stage of Socialism.

The Fourteenth Congress formulations of the Socialist Market Economy and Deng Xiaoping's Theory laid down elements of a theoretical framework which were widely discussed during Mao's birth centenary celebrations in 1993. The Central Party School led by Hu Jintao, the CASS and Shanghai Academy of Social Sciences published numerous writings on the new theoretical line of Deng. The publication of Deng's *Selected Works* (3 vols.) during the same year was followed by a drive to study Deng's works.

The banner of Deng's Theory like the banner of Mao Zedong Thought during the Cultural Revolution divides the loyalists from the dissidents. It also isolates the ideological critics of the current path of development thus uniting the Dengist forces to pursue the present political line.

Constituting Principles of Deng's Theory

1. *Method: Seeking Truth from Facts*: Rejecting dogmatic formulations derived from texts or foreign models or sayings of great leaders, Deng invoked Mao's method articulated in Yan'an during the Rectification Movement and laid down the principle of 'seeking truth from facts'. As he explained in a speech in 1978 all policies must be based on an evaluation of experience. This may mean breaking completely with conventional ideas and principles which had become outmoded in the course of practice. This he called 'emancipation of the mind' (*jiefang sixiang*). It is this method which Jiang Zemin has described as the quintessence of Deng's Theory. It is this outlook which allows one to make bold experiments, taking risks and correcting policies as one moves toward.

   While this method, as it was in the case of Mao, has enormous possibilities for creative developments in Marxism, we also know that there are no objective tests of truth in such contexts. The party leadership is the innovator as well as the one who proclaims its validity.

2. *Focus on Economic Construction*: Deng's Theory embodies a new understanding of socialism at the scientific level. Stressing the centrality of productive forces in socialism, Deng shifted the emphasis from class struggle to economic development. He rejected the isolationist or closed or partly closed economic system under socialism and promoted structural reform and open door for foreign capital. The transformation of the planned economy to a socialist market economy was the most radical step. A reassessment of institutions such as the market which was regarded as an essentially capitalist institution was Deng's contribution. Are these only applicable to the Chinese experiment in socialism or are they new considerations for socialism anywhere in the world? The other question is as to how it would be different from capitalism? Deng's answer probably would be that with a Communist Party in power it would lead the economic process in the direction of socialism. But then with the rise of capitalist classes in society, the social basis of the Communist Party may have changed during the long process of such development and this would perhaps create a prosperous but unequal, consumerist and immoral society. That is why Mao had argued that mere development of the productive forces was not socialism; it had to create a new human being committed to socialist values. Thus, the problem remains as to the conceptualization of socialism. The mention of building both material and spiritual civilizations and the reference to ethical values in the party programme does not seem to be an adequate guarantee to create conditions of socialist freedom—material, cultural and political conditions of human liberation.
3. *Response to the Changed World Situation*: Jiang Zemin says in his report that Deng's Theory reflects a correct analysis of the features of our times, the successes or failures of the socialist countries, the gains and losses of the developing countries, the trends and conflicts of

the developed countries. Actually, what Jiang meant by this was that Deng had to respond to the period of revival of capitalism in the West and its global drive. Under the regimes of Reagan and Thatcher, Western capitalism recouped greatly while the USSR declined at a rapid pace for domestic and international reasons. The Third World countries were engulfed in serious crises of political instability and economic failures. In this situation, Deng recognized the need to build up the economic strength of China. He grasped the role that 'daily advances of science and technology' played in modern life and economy. Thus, when much of the world was debating the evil effects of modernization, Deng asserted it as China's central objective and made it a basis of mobilizing Chinese people's nationalist sentiments. The programme of quadrupling the 1980 level of China's GNP, doubling that of 2000 by the year 2010, building a comprehensive and modern economy by 2021, the centenary of the founding of the CPC and achieving the status of a developed country with the world's second highest GNP—in 2049, the PRC's centenary—are indeed lofty nationalist ideas to catch up with the West.

This strategy to join the race with the West in Western terms of economic growth, science and technology despite the repeated protestations about the Chinese characteristics has its cost. The adoption of the framework of the industrial revolution on the claim that it was a universal force and not typical of capitalism has serious implications. It is a sure way to assimilate China into the global capitalist system.

4. *Special Situation of China*: It is interesting that while the first three elements of Deng's Theory are presented in universalist terms without, however, openly claiming its universal applicability, the fourth point in Jiang's report refers to 'the scientific system of building socialism with Chinese characteristics'. He says, for the first time it has given preliminary but systematic

> answers to a series of basic questions concerning the road to socialism in China, the stages of development, the fundamental tasks, the motive force, the external conditions, the political guarantee, the strategic steps, the Party leadership, the forces to be relied on and the reunification of the motherland.

It is claimed that dealing with these issues had produced a 'fairly complete scientific system' which is called Deng's Theory which, of course, needs to be 'further enriched and developed'.

No doubt it is a new package of guiding policies. But it was still evolving as a package. It required Deng's personal intervention first in mid-1989 when he called in the PLA to crush youth demonstrations and then in early 1992 when in the course of his Southern Tour he called for further reform and opening and accelerated growth. Therefore, the comparison with the 1945 Seventh Congress articulation of Mao Zedong Thought with the Fifteenth Congress formulation on Deng's Theory may be somewhat unnatural even though both statements summed up about twenty years' political practice. However, it should be noted that in both cases chosen objectives had been substantially attained: Mao's new democratic revolution and Deng's economic development or socialism with Chinese characteristics as conceptualized by Deng.

9

Jiang Zemin's Three Represents

Hu Jintao, as general secretary of the Communist Party of China, and his colleagues, who constitute the party's fourth generation leadership, were armed by Jiang Zemin with a new ideological tool called *Sange Daibiao* (The Three Represents) which, like Deng Xiaoping's *Gaige Kaifang* (Reform and Open) Door), seems to be slowly capturing the imagination of the Chinese as a departure from Marxism. The right is equally disappointed by the refusal to grant full freedom to the propertied classes. Yet the Three Represents are carefully crafted guidelines for the party to face the challenges of the emerging world and to take the country forward in the new century.

The 16th National Congress of the Communist Party of China held in November 2002 and the first session of the 10th National People's Congress of (March 5-18, 2003) installed a new leadership in China which was described as the fourth generation in the history of the CPC. The important thing to note is that it was not merely a new generation in terms of age, but it was also a generation of relatively younger professionals that was handed down a new ideological formulation. Hence this transition had two major dimensions, though interconnected. First was the political transition in party leadership from Jiang Zemin who represented the third generation after Mao Zedong, the leader of the Chinese People's Democratic Revolution, and Deng Xiaoping, the architect of China's reforms, to Hu Jintao, CPC's new general secretary symbolizing the coming of the fourth generation. Second was the adoption of a new ideological formulation called the 'important thought (*zhuyao sixiang*) of Three Represents' (*sange daibiao*) into the constitution of the CPC and the political discourse of the new Chinese leadership. Both these measures were accompanied by a visionary statement by outgoing general secretary Jiang Zemin to build a 'well-off society' (*xiaokang shehui*) in an 'all-round way' (*chuanmian*) which included, besides a strategy of comprehensive development, a specific economic target of doubling the GDP per capita of 2000 by 2010 and doubling it further by 2020.[1]

At the 10th NPC a new set of state leaders succeeded president Jiang Zemin (age 76) and premier Zhu Rongji (75). As expected the new party leader Hu Jintao (60) moved into the office of the president while Wen Jiabao (also 60) who was a senior vice-premier in the outgoing State Council became the new premier. Zeng Qinghong (63) the former party secretary of Shanghai became the new vice-president—a post held by Hu Jintao for the last five years. The successor to Li Peng (75) as NPC Standing Committee chairperson became Wu Bangguo (60) also with work experience in Shanghai. The United Front organ Chinese People's Political Consultative Conference (CPPCC) which is a gathering of non-communist parties and groups is usually also headed by a member of the CPC Politburo Standing Committee. Jia Qinglin (62) from Hebei province who had been in charge in Fujian earlier had been assigned to this post on the retirement of Li Ruihuan (69). Jiang Zemin retained with him the position of the chairman of the Central Military Commission both of the party and the state as Deng Xiaoping had done from 1979 till 1990. Jiang, therefore, continued to have a certain guiding role for the next few years. But clearly a new team had taken charge. Both president Hu Jintao and premier Wen Jiabao announced their new tasks on the concluding day of the 10th NPC while affirming continuity of the basic policies. President Hu praised Jiang Zemin's 'able leadership and his outstanding contribution to the building of socialism with Chinese characteristics' and pledged to carry on his policies.[2] Premier Wen was equally appreciative of his predecessor Zhu Rongji's contributions from whom he said there was 'much to learn'. Wen also announced his four-point plan of work.[3]

The smoothness of this peaceful political transition from an older generation has been rightly appreciated inside and outside China. A key to the understanding of this transition is the new ideological formulation which contains in it the political response of the third generation leadership to the socio-political problems of the past decade while passing on the responsibility to the next generation. Thus the new slogan of building a 'well-off society in an all-round way' and the idea of the Three Represents which were frequently mentioned both in the Party Congress as well as the NPC in effect serve as the political link between the third and the fourth generations. Just as Jiang Zemin's Political Report to the 16th Party Congress did in November, Premier Zhu's Report on the Work of the Government to the 10th NPC as well as Hu Jintao's concluding speech at the latter put Deng Xiaoping theory and the important thought of Three Represents as the guide for both the party and the state. The fuller implications of the ideological stand of the CPC's fourth generation leadership can be grasped if we put it in a historical perspective and identify the recent political context. Before that let us look at the components of the new idea.

Three Represents

The idea of Three Represents can be seen either as a rationalization of the policies which have already unfolded in China during the preceding 13 years under the leadership of Jiang Zemin or a creative development of the CPC's ideological line carrying the stamp of the retiring leader. It could also be seen as a combination of both.

In either case this new formulation has emerged as the ideological line handed down by Jiang Zemin to the fourth generation following a prolonged process of consensus-building. Each principle in the idea of the Three Represents and the three principles as a set have serious implications for the CPC's perspective on economic, political and social policies that have evolved in recent years. The political significance of the Three Represents lies in the fact that they are expected to maintain continuity between the present set of policies and the future while at the same time enabling the new leadership to evolve new policies as it 'advanced with the times' as Jiang did in his time and Deng did before him in innovating new policies.

The amendment to the party constitution adopted by the 16th Congress on November 14, 2002 announced that the party represents the

(1) development trend of China's advanced productive forces (*xianjin shengcanli*)
(2) orientation of China's advanced culture (*xianjin wenhua*)
(3) fundamental interestes of the overwhelming majority of the Chinese people (*zhueda duoshu rende genben liyi*)

This was added to the already existing formulation on the character of the party which itself had undergone important modifications under Mao Zedong and Deng Xiaoping. Instead of only saying as per the formulation of the *Communist Manifesto* of 1848 and reiterated by Lenin and Stalin that the Communist Party was the vanguard of the working class, the CPC under Mao was also described as representing the core of the Chinese people. Under Deng the Chinese nation was added to Chinese people and the working class. Thus the 15th Congress of the CPC in 1997 which had met after the death of Deng and had put his ideas into the party constitution had said: 'the CPC is the vanguard both of the Chinese working class and the Chinese people and the Chinese nation as well as the core of leadership for the cause of socialism with Chinese characteristics.' To that formulation the 16th Congress added the third principle of the Three Represents.[4]

The idea of the Three Represents is clearly associated with the name of Jiang Zemin and the party resolution explicitly says as much referring to the valuable experience since Jiang took over the leadership in June 1989 at the Fourth Plenum of the 13th Central Committee. That was when Deng Xiaoping named him, then the Shanghai party secretary, to the post of the general secretary after the Tiananmen demonstrations were suppressed. It was acknowledged that in course of running the party and the state for nearly 13 years Jiang had formed this 'important thought of Three Represents'. Put in the framework of Deng

Xiaoping, this idea is based on the practice of building socialism with Chinese characteristics under Jiang Zemin and 'a deeper understanding of what socialism is, how to build it and what kind of party to build and how to build it'.[5] In other words, Three Represents provides a guiding perspective for almost all actions of the party and the state. No wonder therefore, we find that starting from Hu Jintao almost all the important leaders mention the new 'mantra' as a reference point since it was formalized at the party congress.

Ideas of Mao, Deng and Jiang Zemin

The revised CPC Constitution mentions Marxism-Leninism Mao Zedong Thought and Deng Xiaoping Theory and the Important Thought of Three Represents as its guide to action. In practice, however, the latest component of the theoretical formulation has always been the relevant guiding framework for the CPC. Mao Zedong Thought was Marxism-Leninism applied to the Chinese conditions. There were, of course, many interpretations of Mao's thought. During the Cultural Revolution at the height of revolutionary excitement it was considered to be the 'Marxism-Leninism of the era in which imperialism was doomed to be heading towards a total collapse and socialism was advancing towards a worldwide victory'. This interpretation was rejected by Deng Xiaoping after Mao's death. He, however, led the party to retain the significance of Mao's theory of New Democratic Revolution, hence under his leadership the CPC's ideology spoke of Marxism-Leninism Mao Zedong Thought.

Deng, however, evolved many new theoretical formulations in the course of the reforms that he carried out in post-Mao China. Socialist Market Economy and Building Socialism with Chinese Characteristics were the two major formulations which embodied his new principles. The reforms in the ownership structure that heralded household responsibility system in China's agriculture and market principles guiding the entire economy and opening of China to foreign investment were rationalized under these ideological principles. Early in the reforms period Deng had not only announced a 'central focus' (*zhongdian*) of all activity of the party and the state on 'economic construction' but also Reforms and the Open Door as the overall strategy for modernization. In March 1979 he had also announced Four Cardinal Principles as guiding the Party: They were: (1) Keep to the Socialist Road, (2) Uphold the Dictatorship of the Proletariat, (3) Uphold the Leadership of the Communist Party and (4) Uphold Marxism-Leninism Mao Zedong Thought.[6] After Deng's death the CPC christened these ideas as Deng Xiaoping Theory (*lilun*) for building Socialism with Chinese Characteristics at the 15th Party Congress. Since then Deng Xiaoping Theory became the ideological banner applying Marxism-Leninism Mao Zedong Thought to China's contemporary realities.[7]

It is in course of applying Deng's Theory to the present-day tasks that Jiang Zemin came up with his idea of the Three Represents. Undoubtedly there is an element of historical recognition of Jiang's performance for as long as 13 years guiding China's successful strides in economic growth, political stability and global prestige. As he passed on the baton of leadership to Hu Jintao, Jiang made sure that Three Represents entered the Party Constitution and common people's vocabulary. Yet he had a modest claim on the status of the formulation, namely, 'important thought' without linking his personal name with them, though others routinely associate it with him. For Deng it was Theory (*lilun*) and for Mao it was Mao Zedong Thought (*sixiang*). The term Ism (*zhuyi*) was reserved only for the founders of communism, Marx and Lenin.[8]

There were indications that the idea of the Three Represents did not have smooth sailing. There were some colleagues of Jiang Zemin in the old Politburo Standing Committee such as Li Ruihuan who were not very enthusiastic about the theoretical significance of the concept. Some were clearly opposed to the idea for its negative political implications. But Hu Jintao as the president of the Central Party School and the principal party theoretician had indeed stood by Jiang Zemin. It is said that Hu was the one who had helped formulate the Deng Xiaoping Theory as well in 1997. This time too he had probably a hand in articulating Jiang's idea of the Three Represents.

Jiang Zemin publicly mentioned the Three Represents in a speech on January 25, 2000 during an inspection tour of Guangdong Province.[9] Emphasizing that the party was facing a new situation with the onset of the 21st century he called upon the party to prepare itself to meet the new challenges. In the subsequent months Jiang talked about the Three Represents on many occasions. The idea attracted worldwide attention when he dwelt upon it extensively at the speech celebrating the 80th anniversary of the founding of the CPC on July 1, 2001.

Jiang grounded his argument in all his speeches mainly on two points. First was the new historical situation that the party faced domestically and internationally. At home the reforms had achieved many successes, but some new problems too had come up such as structural imbalances in the economy, regional disparity and social problems including rising inequality and corruption. Internationally, economic globalization and the strategic environment of the post-cold war era had posed new challenges. Second, the new situation needed innovations in the 'theoretical system, scientific and technological'. Jiang said in a speech in June 2000: 'We must respect the truth and be bold enough to make new innovations, so as to push forward all works of the party and the country'.[10] He added, 'to make theoretical innovations is to push forward our party's basic theories through absorbing new practical experience and new ideas while inheriting the good things of the past.' Not only did Jiang base his own theory on Deng's many new concepts which was politically very important for gaining legitimacy, he also quoted from Mao's 1937 essay 'On Practice' in support and cited Mao's theory of New Democratic Revolution as an innovation. Jiang tried to present his own theoretical innovation in the same series of CPC's creative ideology.

The second point on which Jiang grounded his idea of Three Represents was connected with the emerging political economy of China and its new social forces. New classes had come up both in the city and the countryside with the growth of the market economy. They were not only competing for wealth and influence but were making demands on the party and the state. Their activities were on the one hand part of the economic success story of contemporary China, while on the other hand they were linked with the global market and communication network. The challenge for the party was how to cope with these forces. Should they be allowed to develop their own political organizations and compete with the CPC? Or was it preferable to make an opening in the party for some of these forces?

It is this proposal to open party membership to entrepreneurs which came under scrutiny within China and abroad. In the 80th anniversary speech in July 2001 Jiang explained the nature of the new social strata which had emerged in the multiple systems of ownership in the socialist market economy. There are, among others, 'entrepreneurs and technical personnel employed by the scientific and technological enterprises of the non-public sector, managerial and technical staff employed by the foreign-funded enterprises, the self-employed and private entrepreneurs, employees in the intermediaries and freelance professionals… this new strata have contributed to the development of the productive forces and other undertakings in the socialist society through honest labour and work or lawful business operations. They join workers, farmers, intellectuals, cadres and PLA officers and men in an effort to build socialism with Chinese characteristics.' Hence it is 'also necessary to accept those outstanding elements from other sectors of the society who have subscribed to the party's Programme and the Constitution…and proved to meet the requirements for the party's membership through a long period of tests.'[11] A very important view reinterpreting the class origins of party members was stated by Jiang thus: 'It is not advisable to judge a person's political orientation simply by whether he or she owns property, and how much property he or she owns. But rather, we should judge him or her mainly by his or her political awareness, moral integrity and performance...'[12]

Since this approach represented a major change in the membership policy of the party it was bound to generate a debate. It was reported that during the annual retreat of the party at Beidaihe in August 2001 there were heated exchanges over whether Three Represents should be adopted by the party documents. Inner-Party debates continued throughout the period till the next year's retreat. Eventually, Jiang Zemin and the Shanghai group as well as Hu Jintao achieved maximum support in favour of the ideological formulation as a part of the package negotiated among the various leaders old and new. It was reported that one of the reasons for the delay in the convening of the 16th Congress in November rather than earlier as scheduled was the differences over the Three Represents entering the party Constitution, besides the foreign trips that Jiang was to undertake. It became entangled in the process of bargaining for the smooth transition from and retirement of Jiang Zemin. In the end Jiang accomplished his goal and the new Politibureau got committed to the Three Represents.

Productive Forces, Culture and People's Interest

An examination of the three specific formulations in the Three Represents shows a number of political dimensions of the ideology of the fourth generation. The focus on economic growth that Deng Xiaoping had chalked out in 1978 and Jiang Zemin had continued remained untouched. That is connected with China's rise as a world power and hence is a constant boost to Chinese nationalism. While the first principle stresses the centrality of the productive forces, the second relates it to culture, so that the criticism against excessive materialism and hedonism and 'worship of money' in today's China is met. The third principle is about representing the people's interest. At one end it signifies democratic procedures and the accountability of the party to the masses while at another end it seeks to widen the party's support base. This is how Jiang Zemin makes an attempt to win over the new social strata that previously found it difficult to enter the party and even saw the party in a hostile manner. Thus the Three Represents are a package of economic, social and political guidelines which rationalize some of the policies that the CPC had already begun to pursue in the past two decades. At the same time they are presented in a framework of Marxism in the modern conditions obtaining in China as creative formulations.

In his Report to the 16th Congress Jiang Zemin discusses the three Represents in the section on 'Strengthen and Improve

Party Building' and treats it as necessary for improving the party's 'art of leadership and governance'. He called upon especially senior and middle rank cadres to "emancipate their minds", i.e. stop questioning this formulation. He urged them to "keep pace with the times and boldly engage in practice and innovation".[13] Such innovations are needed by the party according to Jiang to take the people along as otherwise the gap between the people and the party will grow. This is clearly a response to the growing demand for democratic rights in various spheres in China. The other massive challenge is the phenomenon of corruption. Jiang said: "If we do not crack down on corruption the flesh-and-blood ties between people and the party will suffer a lot and the party will be in danger of losing its ruling position, or possibly heading for self-destruction." The building of a spiritual civilization on a code of ethics as indicated in the second principle is one check to constantly remind the cadres of "China's advanced culture". People's supervision and accountability are envisaged in the third principle provided there are institutional checks on decision-making to ensure that the decisions are in the interest of the "overwhelming majority". There is a reiteration of the CPC's famous commitment to the "mass line" in the Report.[14] But obviously it needed to be further concretized in practice. Clearly at this point of history the party realizes the magnitude of the problems facing it and through these formulations it seeks to evolve a framework to respond to them and "improve its governance capacity". Incidentally, the term 'governance' has also become popular in contemporary China, reflecting its assimilation with the dominant discourse on globalization.

The first of the Three Represents, advanced productive forces, carries forward the Deng idea that science and technology are the primary productive forces, therefore a critical tool to lead modernization of agriculture, industry and all other sectors. Now it comes in handy for dealing with the tasks of economic globalization that stress free movement of capital and technology because China remains underdeveloped in vast sectors of production. Undoubtedly it has travelled a long distance from the Maoist idea of continuation of class struggle in socialist society. But the real problems of social inequality, regional disparity and unequal trade continue to haunt the policy-makers of China. How to remain committed to some of the basic values of socialism while being mainly engaged in "increasing the overall national strength and improving people's living standards" is a major task for the fourth generation.

The second principle about the party representing advanced culture is supposed to be an answer to the above dilemma. Jiang said in 2001: "...to develop advanced culture means to develop a socialist culture with distinctive Chinese characteristics and build socialist spiritual civilization".[15] Is it a reminder of the great Confucian values, ethical standards which have inspired the Chinese for centuries? Is it a call for absorbing the best of world culture? There is no direct answer to these questions. Almost recalling Mao Zedong's discussion on culture in 'On New Democracy' in 1940, Jiang asked for developing a "national, scientific and popular socialist culture"—socialist was an addition in this case. The reference to scientific culture makes it global. Indeed, the May Fourth Movement legacy was reaffirmed along with "all the advanced civilization achievements mankind has ever created".[16] As for ancient Chinese culture there is reiteration of the fact that the party had "cleaned up the old decadent and dying culture which was left over from the old society or infiltrated into China from abroad". That, of course, is a big assumption which can be questioned. In any event, according to Jiang Zemin developing a socialist culture is to "turn people from generation to generation into citizens with lofty ideals, moral integrity, better education and good sense of discipline".[17] There was a great deal of emphasis on promoting "scientific approaches and scientific thinking" which is relevant in the wake of the campaign against cults such as Fa Lun Gong. The central theme that Jiang stressed was promotion of socialist culture accompanied by some of the Mao era ideas—"serve the people" and "let a hundred flowers blossom and let hundred schools of thought contend". The latter was a slogan from ancient China revived in 1956 as a principle for democratic debates, but sometimes was followed by suppression of the critics. It should be pointed out that soon after the 16th Party Congress the campaign on Learn from Lei Feng in serving the people was revived. Hu Jintao visited poorer regions like Shaanxi and affirmed the party's and his own commitment to serving the masses. But subjective declaration of commitments is one thing and objective processes initiated by the market economy are another. These value assertions seem to be directed at the milieu of cut-throat competition in present-day China and actually Mr. Money (*Qian Xiansheng*) happens to be the most powerful cultural force in present-day China.

Creativity and Nationalism

The third principle concerns the fundamental interests of the overwhelming majority and this is CPC's answer to the demands of democratization together with the first two. The first provides the material conditions for democracy by providing decent livelihood conditions. The second gives the cultural support in terms of rational and ethical values. This one calls upon the party to take "fundamental interests as the starting point" and ensure to the people "continued tangible economic, political and cultural benefits on the basis of steady social development and progress." According to Jiang, the overall interests of the people are composed of specific interests of people from different quarters and therefore the interests of different classes and ethnic groups have to be fulfilled. There is no detailed discussion in theoretical terms of the class, ethnic, gender and regional differentiation of the Chinese people and how to fulfil their specific needs. We, of course, know that there is the Western Region Development Plan, Poverty Eradication Policies, Women Federation's various programmes and the new policies on social security for the unemployed and others. Both Hu Jintao and Wen Jiabao have shown serious interest in these areas even in the first weeks of their installation. But the CPC's ideological perspective is still not directly sensitive to the specific demands of differentiated groups. From the Four Class United Front of the People's Democratic Revolution, the party moved to the macro perspective of the Chinese people of all nationalities and the present formulation on the overwhelming majority continues that perspective. No doubt, it alerts itself on the question as to whether by being identified with the interest of the rich and the upcoming entrepreneurs and the professionals it was getting more and more isolated from the common people. How to avert that is the question. Jiang says that leading cadres should keep in mind the security and well-being of the people and show concern for people's sufferings. How is that to be different from a patronising role by the party authorities unless people exercise their rights through institutions and movements? The CPC has steadily enlarged the legal-institutional framework of decision-making by enacting many new laws and operating the people's congress system at various levels. Jiang emphasizes the significance of political reforms to "develop people's democracy" under socialism. In the Report to the 16th Congress he, however, rejects "copying of any model of the political systems of the West" while affirming the agenda of institutional improvement. [18] Self-governance at the village level, at the level of Residents Committees in cities and the operation of Workers Representative Conferences in enterprises are mentioned. But the report gives no indication of raising the multicandidate elections to the township level in the countryside. Yet we know that in some places already such elections have taken place and there may be a gradual process of competitive election from below. However, for Deng Xiaoping's heirs the guiding principle is that the political process must serve the need for social stability which is necessary for economic development of China. But there is no doubt that political reforms for greater democracy at every level is very much a part of the contemporary discourse in China. Some intellectuals have talked about developing a third civilization – a political civilization in addition to the material and spiritual civilizations.[19] The new political civilization is not necessarily conceptualized in liberal democratic terms, but in a framework of creative development of people's democracy seeking comprehensive, multi-demensional freedom.

CPC general secretary Hu Jintao and his colleagues who constitute the fourth generation leadership of the Chinese have been armed by Jiang Zemin with a new ideological tool called *Sange Daibiao* (Three Represents) which, like Deng Xiaoping's

Gaige Kaifang (Reform and Open Door) seems to be slowly capturing the imagination of the Chinese people. It is true that this formulation is seen by the Left as an outrageous departure from Marxism as it dispenses with the issue of exploitation of labour by capital and the principle of the party being the vanguard of the proletariat. The Right is equally disappointed by the refusal to grant full freedom to the propertied classes. At the same time the Three Represents are carefully crafted guidelines for the party that is determined to face the challenges of the emerging world and take the country forward in the new century. It is an "important thought" that rationalizes some important policies and practices and charts out a course of development. Updating of principles to face new situations always involves a creative exercise. But one is not certain if it is a case of creative development of Marxist ideology as the philosophical principles underlying the three ideas have not been worked out in any depth in a new way. In fact intellectuals are yet to take it as a serious theoretical formulation. That does not reduce its political significance at all. It is meant to point to the road towards building a "well-off China in an all-rounded way". It may be recalled that "rich country and strong nation" (*fuguo qiangzu*) was a late 19th century banner in China which caught the imagination of the Chinese people for over a century. Sun Yat-sen's Three People's Principles (People's Nationalism, People's Livelihood and People's Rights) and Mao Zedong's People's Democratic Revolution carried forward the same message in the first three quarters of the 12th century in their respective ways. Deng Xiaoping was clearly focused on those objectives. Jiang Zemin had put into practice Deng Xiaoping Theory under that longstanding banner of Chinese nationalism. Three Represents as the ideological statement of the fourth generation CPC leaders underline the nature of the achievements and the problems facing them as much as challenging Hu Jintao and Wen Jiabao to constantly review as to whether the current policies fulfil the aspirations of Chinese nationalism as well as Chinese revolution in the 21st century.

NOTES

1. On the conclusion of the 10th NPC the new prespective was clearly evident in the CPC organ's editorial 'Embark on the Great Journey of Building a Well-off Society in an All-Round Way' *People's Daily*. March 19, 2003.
2. Speech at the Closing Session of the 10th NPC, *People's Daily on-line* (March 19, 2003).
3. Wen Jiabao's statement at his first press conference on March 18, 2003 in *People's Daily* (March 19, 2003). Wen's four points referred to reforming the rural economy, state-owned enterprises, the financial system and government agencies.
4. 'Resolution on the Amendment to CPC Constitution,' *News from China*, vol. xv. no. 2, (January 16-31, 2003), p. 11.
5. Ibid., p. 11.
6. "Uphold the Four Cardinal Principles", *Selected Works of Deng Xiaoping (1975-1982)* (Beijing: Foreign Languages Press, 1984), p. 172.
7. Manoranjan Mohanty, 'The New Ideological Banner: Deng Xiaoping Theory', *China Report,* vol. 34, no. 1 (January-March 1995). Chapter 8 in this volume.
8. For a discussion of this see Manoranjan Mohanty, 'Power of History: Mao Zedong Thought in Deng's China', *China Report* vol. 31, no. 1 (January-March 1995). Chapter 7 in this volume.
9. Jiang Zemin, *On the 'Three Represents'* (Beijing: Foreign Languages Press, 2001), p. 7.
10. Ibid., p. 59.
11. Speech at the 80th Anniversary Celebration, in ibid., p. 201.
12. Ibid., p. 201.
13. Jiang Zemin's Report to the 16th Congress of the CPC (Beijing: Foreign Languages Press), November 2002, Section X 1.
14. Ibid., Section X 4.
15. Speech at the 80th Anniversary Celebration, op. cit., p. 187.
16. Ibid., p. 190.
17. Ibid., p. 188.
18. Jiang Zemin's Report, op. cit., Section V 1.
19. Lecture by Bai Lichang, Professor of Philosophy, Shaanxi Academy of Social Sciences at the Institute of Social Sciences, Delhi on March 7, 2003.

10

China's Focus on Governance

Governance as a concept is no longer confined to the discourse on globalization or prescriptions by multilateral institutions such as the World Bank for implementation of administrative reforms and promotion of transparency and accountability. The Communist Party of China (CPC) adopted a major resolution to "enhance governance capability" *(jiaqiang zhizheng nengli)*, while completing the leadership transition from Jiang Zemin, 78 to Hu Jintao, 61. The new leadership of China has chosen to focus on governance on the reasoning that the CPC continuing to exercise power in China depended on it. There were indications of this line of thinking even at the 16th Party Congress in November 2002 when Hu succeeded Jiang as CPC general secretary. After Hu Jintao took over as president of China from Jiang and Wen Jiabao as premier from Zhu Rongji in 2003, the new team, known as the fourth generation leadership (Mao, Deng Xiaoping and Jiang representing the first three generations) had begun to embark on a new style of political functioning. Confronting the outbreak of SARS soon after coming to power was their first major test and they had many lessons to learn from the experience. At the Fourth Plenum of the Central Committee from September 16 to 19, the Hu-Wen leadership not only worked out the succession process, but also launched the drive to streamline governance. This latter decision was as important as the resignation of Jiang Zemin, from the chairmanship of the Central Military Commission (CMC), which was preceded by a lot of speculation.

It was reported that Jiang wished to continue in the post of the CMC chairman to continue his military reforms and pursue the stated policy on Taiwan. He had considerable backing within the party, including from military leaders. Hu Jintao had to prepare the ground to pressurize Jiang to retire by various means. The anti-corruption campaign against party figures and the sons and daughters of leaders was strengthened, touching in the process some known favourites of Jiang Zemin such as the singer Song Zuying. The management of military affairs during Jiang's regime also came for critical discussion within the party, including his manner of dealing with the US. The celebrations of the Deng Xiaoping birth centenary as well as the fiftieth anniversary of the founding of the National People's Congress were used to give hints to Jiang to resign and promote an institutional functioning of the party and the state.

Jiang Zemin's letter of resignation dated September 1, 2004 is unambiguous about his desire to retire and hand over the office to Hu Jintao who is 'competent and qualified'. Therein he also stated that he had expressed his desire to retire from all these posts before the Sixteenth Party Congress in 2002 and the party had decided to continue this arrangement until now, in view of the challenges of the domestic and international situation. But Jiang said there should be "absolute leadership of the party over the military" and therefore his resignation should be accepted.

In any case, the Hu Jintao leadership has managed the political transition fairly well. The promotion of Xu Caihou, instead of Jiang's protégé Zeng Qinghong, as a vice-chairman of the CMC showed a clear consolidation of Hu's power. Xu had worked in the Shenyang Military Region in the north-east for many years before becoming the executive deputy director of the PLA's General Political Department and member of the CMC in 1999. Four additional members—Chen Bingde, Qiao Qingchen, Zhang Dingfa and Jiang Zhiyuan, all military leaders —were added to the commission raising its strength to 11.

But the supposed sidelining of Zeng Qinghong may be an exaggeration. Zeng was not only the vice-president of China, he was also the secretary in charge of the party secretariat as well as the president of the party school—a position that Hu held before him. So it is perhaps a collective leadership of the party, with responsibility of the government with premier Wen Jiabao and the party organization with Zeng Qinghong, under the overall leadership of party general secretary Hu Jintao. It was Zeng who presented the all-important resolution on 'Enhancing Governance Capability of the Party' at the Fourth Plenum and explained its provisions. The collective posture is also evident from the fact that while the earlier reference to the leadership from 1989 till 2002 mentioned the central committee with "Jiang Zemin as the core", the current formulation refers to the central committee with "Hu Jintao as the general secretary". In general, Wen Jiabaos got no less publicity in the press than Hu. In fact, Wen acquired a great deal of popularity because of his approachability, relaxed manners and frequent interaction with common people. At the same time, Hu's image of being a leader with considerable responsiveness to people's problems has also crystallized.

With Hu Jintao's leadership established in all three realms of power in the party, state and the army, the new team lost no time to launch the initiative to reform the party's functioning. The context of this new initiative is a deep anxiety about the unfolding trends in China, keeping in mind the lessons from the collapse of the Soviet Union and the apprehension of 'peaceful evolution of capitalism'—both of which present worrying scenarios for the Chinese leaders. But the fact that the CPC leadership has undertaken this exercise shows their self-confidence and determination to tackle the daunting problems. Despite the economic successes during the 25 years of economic reforms, recording an average of over 7 per cent annual rate of growth and achieving US$ 1,000 per capita income, China is facing many serious challenges.

The Development and Reforms Commission of China's State Council asked 98 well known Chinese and foreign experts to name the risk factors which should be kept in mind while preparing the Eleventh Five Year Plan for 2006–10 (*People's Daily* online, August 31, 2004). They listed 10 major problems: (1) *Unemployment*, (2) Problems relating to farmers, countryside and agriculture (*nongmin, nongcun, nongyeh* – the much talked about *san nong* or 'three rural' issues – agriculture having become unprofitable and farmers' income becoming stagnant which has caused rural discontent (3) *Financial sector* adversely affecting capital flow, (4) *Rich-poor gap* having crossed the international 'red line', (5) *Environmental problem,* especially water and air pollution, and a shortage of water resources affecting people's health, (6) *The Taiwan* issue assuming critical proportions, (7) *Globalization* creating uncertainties despite the high rate of foreign investment, (8) Capacity to tackle crisis related to *corruption,* an underdeveloped legal system, the relation between party and the masses and decline in the legal authority of the government, (9) Problem of *confidence and credibility* evident in corruption by government officials and perversion of social mores reflected in the credit transactions in China, and finally (10) *AIDS and public hygiene*—apprehension of not 10 million but as many as 30 million AIDS patients in the near future. SARS in 2003 brought to light the dimensions of the lack of public hygiene and the poor health system.

This random list of problems suggests the intensity of the crisis that may manifest itself in China. As for the capacity of the party cadres to handle a possible crisis, another recent survey by the party school gave startling findings. Out of the party's leading cadres above the county level, more than half of those surveyed lacked the ability to "make a scientific judgment of a situation" while more than one-third "had difficulty in tackling a complicated situation" or "totally lost their heads" (sic) in such a situation (*People's Daily* online, September 17, 2004. In recent years there has been much talk about incompetent cadres, loopholes in governance and immature mechanisms of governance.

This is why the Fourth Plenum resolution declares that China's reforms and development have reached a critical stage in which new situations and new problems are mushrooming and "hostile forces are still pursuing their strategic attempts to Westernize and separate our country". The latter refers to the push given by some to the pro-independence forces in Taiwan. It warns that "the CPC's ruling status is by no means the natural result of the party's founding and will not remain for ever if the party does nothing to safeguard it." It calls upon the party members to have a 'stronger sense of crisis' and draw lessons from the experiences of other ruling parties in the world.

During the first two years the new leadership popularized the notion of 'people first' in the conduct of government activities. This is consistent with the principle of the party representing the interest of the vast majority of people, which is the third item in Jiang Zemin's idea of Three Represents. Hu Jintao has promoted what he calls the "scientific concept of development", which is comprehensive in nature and which seeks to achieve five balances: rural and urban, coastal and inland regions, social and economic development, economic and ecological development and finally domestic with international. Another assertion of the regime has been to build a "transparent and responsible government". The constitution of the PRC was amended last year to incorporate respect for human rights, the state's obligation to provide social security to citizens and making private property inviolable. This was welcomed by China's growing capitalist class which was already made eligible to join the Communist Party at the 16th Party Congress.

The Fourth Plenum has reiterated the three historic tasks for building a moderately well off society: advancing China's modernization, realizing China's reunification and maintaining world peace and promoting common development of people of the world. Within that perspective, it plans to respond to the emerging problems by affirming the leadership of the Communist Party, emphasizing the people's role in governance and developing rule of law. Yet, Hu Jintao, like his predecessor, has clearly rejected western style democracy and instead has talked about promoting socialist democracy.

Undoubtedly, China's media is freer today than before, but there are still periodic reports of restrictions and dismissals. Publication of independent and critical literature is more frequent than ever before in contemporary China. Yet examples of bans and withdrawal of books are numerous. The recent withdrawal of a very popular 'Survey of Peasants in Contemporary China', which had vividly narrated the plight of the rural areas, was considered unacceptable.

The anti-corruption drive under Hu Jintao is even more aggressive. Tian Fengshan, the former central minister of land and resources, was dismissed from the central committee and the party at the recent Plenum. A number of anti-corruption laws have been passed recently. Summary trials and executions of the convicts continue as before. But the question is whether they are enough measures to cope with the breakdown of the moral order and the spread of the forces of market economy.

China's new generation leaders will very soon realise that governance in the sense of efficient implementation of policy according to rules deals with only a part of the problem. The policies themselves have to respond to the people's concerns. If the policies do not reflect " the scientific notion of development" and do not achieve the balances needed in society then no amount of efficient governance will achieve the goal. The Chinese leaders seem to be aware of this for they do talk about building a 'harmonious society' and simultaneously develop material, spiritual and political civilizations. Jiang Zemin's response to the growing crisis was the Three Represents. His successors are looking for innovative ways to present the 68 million strong CPC before the 1.3 billion people of China as the best bet for their future prosperity and dignity.

11

Hu Jintao's "Scientific Outlook on Development": CPC Grapples with the Success Trap

The 17th Congress of the Communist Party of China (CPC) which concluded its week-long session on October 21, 2007 not only took stock of the many successes China has achieved in the course of three decades of reforms, but paid greater attention to the problems which had arisen in that process. In general secretary Hu Jintao's report these issues were squarely stated and a new perspective called "Scientific Outlook on Development" was articulated as a way out of the dilemmas facing the party and the country today. This was incorporated into the CPC constitution according it a status of a guiding principle. Not only was its application to the main policy areas elaborated, a new central committee was elected by the Congress whose members were selected through a year-long process of investigation on their commitment to pursue scientific development.

Indeed China has accomplished remarkable economic growth since 1978, having quadrupled the per capita national income of 1980 by 2001 and emerging as the world's second largest economy at present. The living standards of the Chinese people have considerably improved and the urban infrastructure in many cities compares with the best anywhere. The rise of China is talked about the world over because of its high rate of growth and increasing influence in world affairs.

But this very success seems to have led China to a series of social, economic and political dilemmas which are not easy to solve. The mode of economic growth has been such that it has created its own momentum, powerful production structures and strong interest groups which have long-term domestic and international commitments. Yet social inequality, regional disparity, environmental degradation and political alienation are growing at such a rate that the prevailing course of development needs urgent reorientation. This is the "success trap" in which China is placed at this current historical conjuncture. Undoubtedly, China has achieved enormous successes, but the manner in which they have been achieved has led it to a trap. The main course of development cannot be reversed, yet the problems have to be addressed.

The significance of the 17th Congress lied in the fact that there is a realization of the magnitude of the crisis and a serious attempt has been launched to get out of the trap. This has been done by shifting the focus from economic growth to "scientific development" that stresses social equity and sustainable development along with growth.

What is Scientific Outlook on Development?

The choice of the word, "scientific" in this formulation does not imply the common sense meaning that would denote a path of development using modern science and technology, even though that is also included in the overall understanding of this concept. This is more in the sense of a scientific perspective that is based on actual experience, considered with care, objectivity, historical knowledge and material evidence. Hu Jintao first mentioned this concept during a visit to Guangdong province during the outbreak of SARS in April 2003 when he asked people to pay attention to a harmonious development of economy and society and to sustainable and all-round development. Thereafter, the concept gradually appeared in party forums. Hu dwelt upon the perspective at length in his pre-Congress ideological session at a national conference of Party leaders at the Central Party School on June 25, 2007, linking it with the concept of building a "harmonious society" and "putting people first" in all aspects of work. In the report to the Congress Hu defines it thus:

The Scientific Outlook on Development takes development as its essence, putting people first as its core, comprehensive, balanced and sustainable development as its basic requirement, and overall consideration as its fundamental approach.

This perspective arises from the realization of serious problems existing in contemporary China. Hu Jintao says that "while recognizing our achievements, we must be well aware that they still fall short of expectations of people". Listing the main difficulties and problems, he says that "our economic growth has been realized at an excessively high cost of resources and environment" and the imbalance in development between urban and rural areas, between regions and between economy and society". Speaking of the crisis facing the farmers he says: "It has become more difficult to bring about a steady growth of agriculture and farmers' incomes". There are problems affecting the immediate interests of people relating to "employment, social security, income distribution, education, public health, housing, work safety, administration of justice and public order and difficult life faced by low income people". There are many empirical evidences to substantiate the seriousness of these problems. The fact that the officially confirmed reports of incidents of mass protest increased from 76,000 in 2004 and 87,000 in 2005 to 1,20,000 in 2006 is a small indication of this situation.

These problems are the cause of disharmony and tensions in society. Therefore Hu Jintao has proposed a new set of policies embodied in this scientific outlook on development to achieve the goal of a "Harmonious Socialist Society"—a goal that was articulated systematically at the sixth plenum of the central committee in 2006 and has now found a place in the CPC constitution. The 16th party congress in 2002 when Hu Jintao succeeded Jiang Zemin gave the slogan of building a "moderately well-off society" by 2020 with a target of quadrupling the GDP. The same goal has been reiterated but with the affirmation of—"a moderately well-off society in an all-round way". Even the growth target has been put in a new perspective of quadrupling the per capita GDP by 2020, not just the absolute volume. Read together with the statement that "development is for the people, by the people and with the people sharing in its fruits" the new perspective certainly amounts to more than the World Bank slogan of "inclusive growth" at least in theoretical terms. Whether the theory makes only symbolic accommodation of the socio-political and environmental challenges, while the market economy maintains its speedy growth because of the very nature of the success trap, only practice will show.

However the CPC leadership under Hu Jintao has clearly made a break with the strategy of breakneck growth that characterized the first twenty years of reforms. It has done so using the familiar method of creatively adapting to the concrete conditions of the changing times. Mao Zedong did it to formulate the theory of people's democratic revolution. Deng Xiaoping called for "emancipation of the mind" to break with Mao's ideas on building socialism. Now Hu Jintao has launched the campaign for a balanced development also by calling for "emancipation of the mind". Right at the beginning of the report Hu says: "Emancipating the mind is a magic instrument (a familiar term again) for developing socialism with Chinese characteristics". Through this process the current leadership has added "scientific outlook on development" to the party constitution after Marxism-Leninism-Mao Zedong Thought, Deng Xiaoping Theory and the Important Thought of Three Represents (Jiang Zemin's formulation), showing its serious commitment to the new policies. As practice shows, the latest formulation is the main guide to current policies.

Thrust of New Policies

The "Reforms and Open Door" policy has been reiterated as it has been responsible for China's rapid development and Hu said to stop or reverse that "would only lead to a blind alley". But there is again and again the mention of overall arrangement of an "all-round economic, political, cultural and social development, balance relations of production with the productive forces and the superstructure with the economic base". In other words, the excessive focus on the economic base may have caused the present problems. That is why the notion of five balances has been stressed. A mechanism will be set up to formulate policies and monitor them to reduce the urban-rural gap and regional disparities. Hu has given a call for promoting the capacity for independent innovation and turning China into an "innovative nation" where scientific and technological innovation is constantly pursued to promote a resource saving and environment-friendly and equitable process of development. For this purpose already a national programme for 2006-20 had been announced.

There is an important decision to bring about transitions in three dimensions of the economy: from relying on mainly investment and export to relying on a well-coordinated combination of consumption, investment and exports, from secondary industry serving as the major driving force to primary, secondary and tertiary industries jointly driving economic growth and from relying heavily on consumption of material resources to relying mainly on advances of science and technology, improvement of the quality of workforce and innovation of management. If these transitions indeed take place in China, then the mainstream economic model that has been propagated since the Western industrial revolution and the technological revolution of building a "knowledge society" will be substantially challenged. The definition of modernization to mean moving from agriculture to industry and then to a service economy is replaced with the notion of comprehensive development. Indeed, China already saw the pitfalls of that strategy by neglecting the rural economy from the early 1990s and focusing on export-led growth. Building a new socialist countryside has now been declared as the "top priority in the work of the whole party". The "three rural problems"—low productivity in agriculture, low income of farmers and low level infrastructure and social facilities in the countryside—have been the subject of close attention during the last four years. Abolition of agricultural tax and many other rural fees have reduced the peasant burden. Many new policies have been announced as a new package to develop the rural economy, including developing the enterprises which were the backbone of rural prosperity in the 1980s. For reducing regional imbalances, in addition to the "Western Region Development Strategy", new programmes for the north-eastern region—an old industrial base built during Japanese occupation and the central region surrounding Wuhan have been announced. The plan is to build several economic rims cutting across provinces and also to develop areas with developed cities as growth poles. One of the most talked about themes in today's China is Hu Jintao's call for spreading a new "conservation culture" and building an energy and environment responsibility system like the production responsibility system based on incentives and disincentives that spurred economic growth during the past three decades. Hu cited the experiences of the previous year when two great lakes of China, Dongting and Taihu were so polluted that the former affected the Yangze river's water in a big stretch of land and the latter led to the suspension of water supply to Wuxi for two weeks. The many mining incidents have been a matter of shame for China. China's carbon emission continues to grow and is a matter of worldwide concern.

The Question of Democracy and Leadership

"People's democracy is the lifeblood of socialism", declares Hu Jintao. Yet the institutional changes in the direction of building a participatory system of self-governance are very few. The one-party rule through people's congresses and a consultative role for the non-communist parties continues to be the pattern. Association of non-communist experts is expanding steadily, including as central ministers. Competitive multi-candidate elections by secret ballot, which was introduced at the village committee level in 1998 however remains the only one of that kind. There is no indication that the present leadership wishes to raise it to the next level (township) in the near future, though more and more cases of townships having competitive elections without intervention are visible.

But Hu Jintao has given a sense of expanded inner-party democracy. The selection of over 2200 delegates to the 17th Party Congress and the election of 204 members and 167 alternates of the Central Committee (CC) and 127 members of the Central Commission of Discipline and Inspection involved a wider consultation and elimination process. The first list of CC candidates had 8 per cent more names and it involved five rounds of elections to get at the final number that was ultimately voted by the Congress. The same goes for the election of the new politburo which has 25 members. The nine-member standing committee of the politburo retains the five top leaders: Hu Jintao re-elected as the general secretary, Wu Bangguo (Chair of the National People's Congress Standing Committee), premier Wen Jiabao, Jia Qinglin (Head of the CPPCC, the United Front organ) and Li Changchun, the ideology and publicity in-charge. The retirement of Vice-President Zeng Qinghong has been regarded as dropping of a rival of Hu. But Hu Jintao was leading a collective leadership anyway. The four new members included two possible successors to Hu and Wen in 2012: Shanghai party secretary Xi Jinping, who in 2002 was 54, Liaoning Party Secretary Li Keqiang, He Guoqiang, head of the CPC Organization Department and Zhou Yongkang, Minister of Public Security.

The Hu Jintao leadership took office on the plank of ushering in a new set of policies centring on equitable and sustainable development, proving a clean and people—friendly administration sparing no efforts to fight corruption and following the same policies on international affairs with a new slogan of building a harmonious world. Whether they will succeed in getting out of the success trap and indeed create material, cultural and political conditions for a harmonious socialist society, only time will tell.

12

Harmonious Society and Beautiful Country: Hu Jintao's Vision and the 18th Party Congress

On November 15, 2012, introducing the new Standing Committee of the Communist Party of China's (CPC) Politburo to the press, Hu Jintao's successor, the new General Secretary Xi Jinping conveyed a crisp message. He put the CPC's mission as rejuvenating the Chinese nation, referring to its five thousand year tradition and focused on the party's tasks of solving people's day-to-day problems of providing adequate employment, education and health and stressed the need to fight corruption. The simple and popular introductory statement by Xi came after a week-long deliberation at the 18th National Congress of the CPC where the centre piece was the outgoing General Secretary Hu Jintao's Report which drew compelling attention of everybody to the compelling attention of everybody to the question that China's path of development had to constantly grapple with questions of social equity and environmental sustainability.

Orienting economic growth to addressing social and regional contradictions in order to build a "harmonious society" and tackling ecological challenges to evolve a "beautiful country" and "changing the growth model" to accomplish those objectives were the themes constantly discussed at the Congress. The slogan of "beautiful country" seriously appeared for the first time during this Congress. The "scientific outlook on development" meaning promoting "comprehensive, coordinated and balanced development" that Hu Jintao has added to the CPC's theoretical perspective during the decade of his leadership was spelt out in even greater detail during this Congress. It was now inscribed into the Party Constitution. But the question that is on everyone's mind is whether Xi Jinping will follow the Hu Jintao line or return to the growth-centric path of Jiang Zemin.

Glorious Decade or Lost Decade?

The 18th Congress was preceded by ban interesting debate in China on the evaluation of the decade of leadership of Hu Jintao and Wen Jiabao, which had assumed office in 2002. While the official media called it a glorious decade, citing achievements on all fronts, in the chat rooms on the internet, in the popular blogs such as weibo, many people called it a lost decade. Many outspoken intellectuals of China freely took this view in their interviews with the foreign media. Hu Jintao was called a "conservative", a status quoist who refused to take bold initiatives in further reforming the state owned enterprises (SOEs) and the financial sector, who allowed the growth rate to slow down from over 10 per cent to about seven per cent. It was pointed out that under this regime mass discontent became even more widespread with as many as 1,80,000 incidents in 2010 and levels of corruption reached new heights. Besides the well-known cases of the expelled Chongqing leader Bo Xilai and his convicted wife Gu Kailai and the in famous instance of the railway minister Liu Zhijun, numerous other cases has been listed as showing how corrupt practices had grown in recent years. It was pointed outthat Hi Jintao was too cautious to disturb the power structure and wanted to complete his tern smoothly. thus from this viewpoint it was a lost decade as China could have achieved much more for its people if only he had vigorously pursued the reforms.

It is this campaign against Hu Jintao's "weak leadership" which enabled the retired leader Jiang Zemin to play an active role in shaping the transition to a new leadership at the 18th Party Congress. China's reformelites who credit Jiang with laying down the framework for a shigh rate of growth, encouraging foreign investment and promoting domestic entrepreneurs to enter the party rallied behind this campaign on the lost decade. This was highlighted globally by the western media. So much so that the whole world waited anxiously to watch whether the new leadership of Xi Jinping would follow the Hu Jintao line of balanced development or get back to the Jiang Zemin path of speedy growth once again. It should be remembered that both Jiang Zemin and his successor Hu Jintao were selected by their common mentor Deng Xiaoping the architect of the reform and open door strategy.

Despite the western media's negative publicity on the performance of the past decade under Hu Jintao, there were objective indicators of China's achievements during this period. China surpassed Japan and became the second largest economy in the world in 2010 and had realised the target of doubling its 2000 level of the gross domestic product (GDP) that year. Under the current projection, it is on its ways to double it again by the year 2020 when it aims at becoming a "moderately well-offsociety"—a target set by Jiang Zemin at the time of his retirement in 2002. Now that goal is described as a "well off society in all respects", carrying the Hu Jintao imprint since 2007. China's coped with the global economic crisis in 2008 by introducing a huge fiscal stimulus package. ($586 billion or RMB 4 trillion) and resumed its growth process was not a small achievement. The successful holding of the Olympics in 2008 and the Shanghai Expo in 2010, on the one hand, and meeting the challenge of the SARS epidemic in 2003 and the Wenchuan earthquake in 2008, on the other, were notable acts of the regime.

But the most important set of measures which have made Hu Jintao popular among the common people were the social security initiatives. Providing subsistence allowance to all those below the poverty line, which was raised, the expansion of the health insurance system to cover almost the whole population, allowance to the urban unemployed, measures to support migrant labour or the floating population in cities, and construction of low-cost housing on a massive scale were some of the conspicuous steps during recent years. The resource saving and environment protection measures under the 11th Five Year Plan (2005-10) and those projected in the 12th Plan have been commendable.

This is the period when the whole world took note of a rising China participating in multilateral organisation, taking a tough stand on conflicts such as in Syria and pursuing clams in South China Sea and so on. In fact, Hu Jintao's Report affirms the task of building up defence commensurate with China's rising status and increasing responsibility in the world. Taking concrete steps to develop China as a maritime power finds prominent place in Hu's Report. In other words, the Hu Jintao regime has continued to pander to the growth of Chinese nationalism and its goal of becoming a great power rivalling the United States. (Even though the Report declares that China would continue to follow its independent foreign policy of peace and development, would never seek hegemony, and the Party Resolution affirms its commitment to the five principles of peaceful coexistence, there is not enough mention in the Report on working for a fair, equitable international order.) Thus on the strengthening of defence forces and taking an active role in regional and international organisations, its accomplishments are evident.

Many Acute Problems

Yet, the decade ended with many acute problems which Hu Jintao acknowledged in his Report.

> Unbalance, uncoordinated and unsustainable development remains a big problem. ...The development gap between urban and rural areas and between regions is still large and so are income disparities. Social problems have, increased markedly There are many problems affective people's immediate interests in education, employment, social security, healthcare, housing, the ecological environment, food and drug safety, workplace safety, public security, law enforcement, administration of justice, etc... Some sectors are prone to corruption and other misconduct, and the fight against corruption remains a serious challenge for us. We must take these difficulties and problems very seriously and work harder to resolve them.[1]

On the whole, the Hu Jintao leadership passes on a legacy of considerable achievement measured even on conventional economic indicators. But its focus was on reorienting the growth strategy towards social equity and environmental sustainability and that is what it embodied in the theoretical formulation on "scientific outlook on development". Formulations such as "putting people first", "handing five imbalances", "harmonious world" and "beautiful country" were bases on that theoretical line. To acknowledge its long term relevance as a guiding principle, the CPC Constitution was amended by the 18th Congress to add this concept to its theoretical set consisting of Marxism-Leninism, Mao Zedong Thought, Deng Xiaoping theory and Three Represents. Describing its as an innovative theory with a Marxist world view that responded to the underlying features of the current times, the "scientific outlook" embodied "what kind of development should China achieve in a new environment and how."[2]

For the whole decade Hu Jintao refrained from affirming his personal leadership in the public media and analysts always referred to the Hu-Wen regime, giving almost equal prominence to Premier Wen Jiabao. But the amended constitution, while inscribing "scientific outlook on development" into its general programme, mentions Hu Jintao as the "chief representative" of the party just as the preceding paragraph mentioned Jiang Zemin in similar terms while mentioning his "important thought of Three Represents."

The political report to the Party Congress and the resolution on amendment to the party constitution were a joint document of the outgoing leadership headed by Hu Jintao and the incoming leadership headed by Xi Jinping. Usually the drafting responsibility is located at the Central Party School of which the president was none other thans the new leader Xi Jinping. Xi had been working as Hu's deputy for the last five years as vice president of the people's Republic of China (PRC). He has the task of reconciling Jiang Zemin's growth perspective with Hu's focus on equity and sustainability. In fact, in his first article as general secretary, published in the *People's Daily* on November 17, 2012, Xi called upon the party to study the "spirit of the 18th

Congress" where the did refer to the "scientific outlook on development."

The new leadership put in place by the 18th Congress clearly reflected the effort to reconcile Jiang Zemin's emphasis on a high growth rate and Hu Jintao's stress on balanced development. Hu Jintao invited over 20 retired leaders to attend the Congress with Jiang given much prominence in public. Many of them also took part in the conventional pre-Congress enclave of leaders at Beidaihe in August where most of the political decisions were worked out. Hu Jintao's consensus building style of decision-making and low-profile demeanour may have appeared to some as "weak leadership". But his role in expelling Bo Xilai and ensuring a smooth transition of leadership and clearly affirming a "scientific outlook on development" as the party's perspective, gave a different message, one of a clear headed-leader.

The New Leadership

The newly elected Standing Committee of the Politburo ofthe CPC had seven members, two less than the outgoing one, apparently for reasons of compactness and cohesion in the crucial decision-making body. All of them had over 20 years of leadership experience at various levels, including top positions in at least two provinces. Besides Xi Jinping, 59 years of age, and Li Keqiang, 57, the other five were in their mid-60s, which meant that as per the age restrictions they would retire at the end of one term, i.e. in 2007. (Since 2002, the unwritten rule governing age restrictions stipulates 70 as the retirement age for national leadership, 67 for provincial leadership) That gives Xi Jinping and Li Keqiang a chance to pick up a set of new leaders who can pursue their plan of action, of whom two would be onthe line of succeeding them five years later in 2022. (It is already noticed that two relatively young leaders are included in the new Politburo. They are Sun Zhengcai 49, until now the Party Secretary of Jilin and transferred to Chongqing succeeding Zhang Dejinag, and Hu Chunhua, also 49, Party Secretary of Inner Mongolia, tipped to take charge of Guangdong.) The new leaders are highly educated not mainly in engineering as in the outgoing Standing Committee, but also in the humanities and social sciences with time spent inthe west. Though Xi Jinping graduated from Qinghua University in chemical engineering he earned a doctorate later from there in Marxist theory. The premier-designate Li Keqiang is an economics graduate from Peking University, also a Ph.D. Both were sent to the countryside as youth during the Cultural Revolution.

Much has appeared in the media about the factional composition of the Standing Committee. Four out of the Seven are supposed tobe nominees of Jiang Zemin and only two of Hu Jintao and one linked to the former premier Zhu Rongji. Indeed, any consensus-building exercise is bound to have such combinations. Xi Jinping, the general secretary and designated to take over as president in the March session of the National People's Congress, Zhang Dejiang, currentvice premier who replaced the dismissed party leader of Chongqing, Bo Xilai, CPC secretaries of Shanghai and Tianjin, Yu Zhengsheng and Zhang Gaoli, these four are said to owe their ascensions to Jiang Zemin. Li Keqiang, who is to succeed Wen Jiabao as premier, came up in the party through the route of the Communist Youth League like Hu Jintao, and Liu Yunshan, the head of the party's propaganda department, both are known to be close to Hu. Wang Qishan, the vice premier, who looked after finance inthe Wen government, is a Zhu protégé who has now been given the responsibility to head the anti-corruption agency of the party, the Central Committee on Discipline and Inspection (CCDI). The western press described Wang as a reform minded leader who had been sidelined to a different kind of job, indicating that the Xi leadership did not want to take strong new measures to carry forward economic reforms. It is premature to read that meassage into this arrangement Li Keqiang himself might play that role, but within the framework agreed upon by the Standing Committee.

The new group, the fifth generation leadership succeeding Mao, Deng, Jiang and Hu] has been seen by many observers as consisting of progenies of former party leaders variously described as "princelings" or "red nobility." The new leader Xi Jinping is the son of Xi Zhongxun, who was one of the prominent revolutionary leaders persecuted during the Cultural Revolution, and as the party leader of Guangdong and member of Politburo in the early reform years, played an important role as a colleague of Deng Xiaoping. Yu Zhengsheng's father, Huang Jing was mayor of Tianjin. Wang Qishan is married to the daughter of Yao Yilin, another reform era leader and vice-premier. The disgraced leader Bo Xilai's father was the famed revolutionary era leader Bo Yibo. But to characterise this element asthe Chinese system's inherent dependence on nepotism and favouritism is an exaggeration. There are far more leaders and cadres who have come up through their grassroots experience. The outgoing leaders Hu Jintao and Wen Jiabao and the incoming premier-designate Li Keqiang are some of the examples. Even the so-called "princelings" have long experience and some of them have stood the test of at least 10 years of public scrutiny as Politburo members or provincial leaders.

The Standing Committee does not have a single woman or a minority nationality representative. The 25 member Politburo, of whom 15 are new, has two women, one more than theprevious one. Beside continuing with the rising star and Fujian province party secretary Sun Chunlan, 62 – moved to lead Tianjin after the Congress. It is inexplicable why Liu or Sun was not included in the Standing Committee. Among the 205 Gentral Committee (CC) members there are 10 from minority nationalities and only nine women. Among the alternate members, however, the proportion is higher, indicating the desire to increase their leadership role in the future. Out of the 171 alternate members, 29 belong to minority nationalities and 20 are women, including minority women leaers (six Dai and eight Mongolian among them). Nearly half of the CC is composed to newcomers, suggesting both continuity and change. The CCDI, headed by Wang Qishan, has 130 members.

Hu Jintao can be credited for organising a smooth institutional transition with several new elements that have earned him admiration. The handing over of the chairmanship of the Genral Military Commission of Xi Jinping has been noticed prominently as his predecessor Jiang Zemin had kept that office with himself fortwo years longer. But equality important was the process that was in operation for at least a year before the Congress. The party units at the grass-roots level were elected with an element of competition and lessening of interference from the higher organs. The number of candidates our of whom delegates to the national congress were to be chosen from the provincial level was further increased from level of the 17th Congress. The 2,270 members of the Congress had 22 per cent women and 11 per cent minority representation.

Yet the party's functioning style was so institutionalized by now that it was unlikely to alter the political parameters set during the past 30 years which they believe had helped in achieving economic growth, managing social and economic crisis and raising China's global standing. The system of choosing leaders at various levels by certain methods of evaluation, and engaging in consultations and deciding on personnel and policy matters by consensus among committee members, is the principle political process evolved in recent years. This system has been characterised by some analysts as China's system of "political meritocracy" embodying elements of the Confucian tradition of rule by those with competence and values. This is not quite the Maoist notion of "red and expert"–a concept that has been abandoned as underlining too much of ideology and less of professionalism during the reform period.

But this system clearly does not meet the requirements of the new environment in China and all over the world in which common people seek self-determination, right to participate in decisions affecting their lives. Hu Jintao acknowledged this in his Political Report in announcing that they would "make people's democracy more extensive, fuller in scope and sounder in practice." However, he declared that while China would learn from the political practices of other countries, it "shall never copy the Western political system." This was also the line of thinking set by Deng Xiaoping and Jiang Zemin.

Hu Jintao emphasised three areas for strengthening democracy First, the system of people's congresses has to function as organs of state power insuch a way that through them people would exercise their "right to participate"—this term is used in the Report—in policymaking and the right to oversight over government and party including courts and "procuratorates" (prosecution agencies). For that purpose there should be more representative from the grass-roots level in them rather than they being dominated by quotas from the party and government. Second, party and government should not interfere in the functioning of the people's congresses. Third, rule of law must be strictly enforced subjecting all party and government cadres to abide by rules so that arenas of discretion in decision-making would be minimised. As before, the 18th Report reiterated the agenda of fighting corruption as an urgent issue, failure in combating which might lead to "the end of CPC rule and collapse of the state." It articulated the "distinctive Chinese approach to combating corruption and promoting integrity by addressing both its symptoms and root causes, combining punishment and prevention, with emphasis on the latter." Unfortunately, these parameters are not very different from what have been in placefor years. They have not prevented large-scale corruption in China including scandals at high levels. The case of Bo Xilai, the dismissed party Secretary of Chongqing illustrated the magnitude of this phenomenon. While he may have represented a challenge to the leadership that succeeded Hu Jintao. The financial dealings and reports of conspiratorial activities exposed serious lapses in the system of governance. The liberalized economy that gives incentives for achieving high targets and showing large profit and the overall decline of moral standards continue to create the climate for illegal financial deals.

Openness in the selection of leaders and a system accountability through checks and balances, even within a framework of "democracy with Chinese characteristics", have to be evolved in China in order to meet the requirements of the new level of democratic consciousness among people. The fear that loosening of authority and control by the central party leadership would lead China toward a Soviet type collapse or that it would reduce its effective capacity for maintaining a high growth rate has actually created an unnecessary appearance of political fragility in what is otherwise seen by many as an efficient political economy delivering results. There may not be an ideal form of democracy anywhere in the world, but each country had to evolve its way of responding to people's urges for self-governance.

Challenges, Civilizational and Political

The new leader, Xi Jinping's principal challenge arises from the perspective on development that Hu Jintao proclaimed in the Political Report and which was inscribed into the amended Party Constitution. The CPC was now committed to trying to achieve economic, political, culturals, social and ecological development *simultaneously.* Affirming all five sectors and putting the ecological dimension at thesame level as the others has been highlighted as the 18th Congress' important message. In the recent two five-year plans, the Eleventh and the Twelfth, resource conservation and environmental protection issues were given concrete shape demanding clear targets and making green assessment of regions, units and leaders obligatory. The new slogan of building a "beautiful country" is the culmination of that process. Yet the carbon emission level remains very high in China and the questionable mentality that economic growth in a developing country had to allow for some pollution to achieve rapid progress still persists in China. Indeed several dam projects were shelved by Wen Jiabao–the Nu River projects in Yunnan, for example–and on the after math of the Congress the press was already carrying reports that the big dam construction lobby hoped for more concessions from the new leadership.

It was Deng Xiaoping who has laid down the guiding principle that "economic construction must betaken as the central point of all work" and that spurred China's economics growth. But he quickly defined the party perspective as one of building a "material and spiritual civilization." His successor Jiang Zemin responded to the new demands for political participation and added "political civilization" to the other two. The 18th Congress took that thinking further to proclaim the five dimensions of development. In 2011, the CPC held its fifth Plenum on culture and formulated a framework that emphasized the need to not only inherit Chinese cultural traditions and share it with the people of the world, but also learn from the plurality of tradition of humanity as a whole. The popularity of western lifestyles and values in China had to be placed in a wider framework without encouraging the assertion of narrow chauvinism flowing from Chinese tradition. That agenda explained later in a July 2012 address by Hu Jintao along with the party's overall programme was far more than laying down a "soft power" strategy of a rising China.

Building of a "harmonious socialist society" that Hu Jintao has put forth as a goal involves working on all the five areas of development so that contradictions did not proliferate, creating causes disharmony. Like the overall perspective of "reform and open door", economic growth was still mentioned as the principal task in the party Constitution on the argument that the productive forces must be developed to provide the material basis for transformation. But unless it was accompanied by social development ensuring improved livelihood, health, education, housing as well as equity and dignity for all individuals and groups and regions, social conflicts were bound to grow.

Overcoming the 'Success Trap'

This is why, in 2011, a major wave of discussion took place in China on "social construction" and "social management" as the new focus of the party. That did not find a prominent mention in the 18th Congress Report, but was in a way integrated into the overall development perspective. Rural-urban disparity and the growing income gap in society was a subject of special in Hu Jintao's Report. Hu called upon industry to help agriculture and the countryside to catch up and thus do in return what the rural sector did earlier to help industrialization to flourish in China. In the backdrop of China currently having one of world's highest levels of inequality of income–nearly 0.5 Gini coefficient with the us; 0.45 and India's 0.36 – Hu Jintao spelt out the need to manage both the primary distribution system (labour, capital, technology and management getting their due share of income) as well as the secondary distribution systems (taxation, social security and transfer payments) through a policy of efficiency and fairness.

During the past decade, all policy documents put economic and social development together. Now equal emphasis had been given to political reforms as well in order to respond to the widespread demand for people's participation, accountability transparency and rule of law applying to all. This was very important at a time when internet access in China and abroad had produced a much freer flow of information in people's demands, exposing cases of corrupting and violations of law by officials. The new cultural agenda of the party had reinvented elements of Chinese civilization that had been relegated to the background and had initiated a fulsome discourse on the literary, cultural, scientific and historical traditions of China and relating them with global traditions, analytically presenting them for creative interpretations through lively debates.

Finally, listing the ecological goal in the same vein as economic and social development completed a train of discourse that Hu Jintao had started in 2003 while defining the party's major agenda of handling the "five imbalances", those between economic and social development, rural and urban, inland and coastal, economy and ecology, and domestic and international sectors. To achieve this goal, affirming the dominant role of the public sector and giving full encouragement to the private sector were both necessary. Maintaining that perspective and carrying it forward will be perhaps Xi Jinping's most formidable task.

To some extent, a few of Hu Jintao's initiative during the past decade took cognisance of some of the main trends in the civilizational movement taking place in the current phase of the global history of humanity. During the past two centuries or more, the epoch of the Industrial Revolution made use of new science and technology to engage in mass production, produced the transition from agriculture to industry and within that from manufacturing to services and then to the knowledge economy. It reorganised rural society into urban and metropolitan centres and defined that process as the inevitable path of civilization progress of humankind. That perspective is increasingly under question in the current age. The notion, no doubt, had its positive elements of human self-development based on reason, human rights and material goods improving livelihood conditions. But it also created notions such as human conquest over nature and control of some groups over others and superiority of some cultures over others as given. That notion of high energy high speed, high consumption and high rise living, defining civilisation's progress, is under severe questioning all over the world today. This is because that path of development has caused a global economic, environmental, political and moral crisis, social and regional inequities and alienation of human beings from one another. Sections of the capitalist world and elites of contemporary China, India and many other countries are trying their best to promote this model of development in the name of globlization. But many social movements in most countries are challenging that model. The 18th Congress of the CPC was caught in the midst of that debate. It called for a "change of the growth model" just as China's Twelfth Plan called for "pattern transformation." But that could have only a narrow meaning asking for reducing the foreign trade component of China's GDP and increasing domestic demand and making investments accordingly and similar structural changes in the existing growth model. It could also mean transforming the essential features of the growth model to achieve the five-dimensions entailed in Hu Jintao's "scientific outlook on development" which could be the key to overcoming China's "success trap"– the economic success of high growth perpetuating the prevailing model which Hu Jintao could not untangle. That is the civilizational-political challenge facing China's new leadership.

NOTES

1. Hu Jintao, "Firmly March on the Path of Socialism with Chinese Characteristics and Strive to Complete the Building of a Moderately Prosperous Society in All Respects", Report to the Eighteenth National Congress of the Communist Party of China on November 8, 2012 (Beijing Xinhua English, 2012-11-17), p. 5.
2. Constitution of the Communist Party of China (Revised and Adopted at the 18th National Congress of the Communist Party of China on November 14, 2012) China org. on November 16, 2012, para 7 in General Programme.

13

Xi Jinping and the "Chinese Dream"

Xi Jinping who had assumed the post of CPC's General Secretary and Chairperson of the Central Military Commission at the conclusion of the Eighteenth Party Congress in November 2012, was elected as the President of the People's Republic of China by the National People's Congress in March 2013. During the early months of his leadership he acquired the reputation of being a practical person who also had the markings of a visionary. From the very start he put emphasis on paying attention to people's concrete day-to-day problems such as jobs, housing, education and health care, also giving a call for cutting down waste of food and giving up ostentatious life style of leaders and cadres and making clean governance and anti-corruption a top priority. At the same time his slogan of fulfilling the "Chinese dream" by 'rejuvenating the Chinese nation' had become the hall-mark of his leadership style.

In this essay we will put the discourse on "Chinese dream" in the context of Xi Jinping's initiatives since he came to power, on the various political, economic and international issues and try to deconstruct the formulation on the Chinese dream. Finally we will assess its political and ideological implications.

Chinese Dream

Xi Jinping first referred to the "Chinese dream" (*zhongguo meng*) in his remarks on 29 November 2012 while visiting the Exhibition on "The Road to Revival" at the National Historical Museum where exhibits depicted the history of China's struggle against humiliation and attacks by colonial powers. He said: "Everyone has his own ideals, aspirations and dreams. Nowadays, the Chinese dream is a hot topic; in my opinion, realizing the rejuvenation of the Chinese nation is the greatest Chinese dream."[1] Since then the talk of the Chinese dream and its various interpretations spread very fast in China. After being elected as President by the National People's Congress Xi mentioned the term nine times in his concluding speech on 17 March 2013 and made 'realising the Chinese dream' the central point of his regime. Thereafter, on every major occasion he referred to the Chinese dream. On the eve of the 92nd anniversary of the founding of the CPC when the Politbureau had a closed door meeting on 22-25 June 2013, he reportedly spelt out his idea in detail, saying that "now the Party and the country are advancing toward completing the building of a moderately prosperous society in all respects and rejuvenation of the Chinese nation."[2]

If the slogan of the Chinese dream is a part of the attempt to prepare the Chinese to work hard to realize the lofty goals set by the Party keeping in view the twin centenaries coming up, the CPC's in 2021 and PRC's in 2049 then there is a clear set of economic priorities. By 2020 they seek to double not only the 2010 GDP but also the per capita income that should reach US$4000.00. By 2040 China is predicted to surpass the GDP level of the US and become the world's largest economy. Way back in the 1980's the architect of China's reforms, Deng Xiaoping had charted out the plan under which China should join the category of middle level developed countries by the middle of the twenty first century. These targets seem eminently achievable under the current pace of change. But the question people are discussing in China is whether the rejuvenation of the five thousand year old Chinese nation meant more than becoming yet another strong military and economic power.

In the recent months the term Chinese dream has become the most frequently used term in the Chinese media. School text-books have been revised to present a discussion on it. There are essay competitions in schools, colleges and the Chinese Academy of Social Sciences has commissioned research projects on this. There are 'Dream Walls' in various places where citizens are encouraged to put up posters - though not quite in the nature of the 'big character posters' of the Cultural Revolution. Folk songs on Chinese dream, some by prominent artists, are played frequently on radio and television.

What exactly does the term 'Çhinese dream' mean ? Is it a mode of nationalist mobilization in support the new leadership of President Xi Jinping and Premier Li Keqiang? Or does it have substantive contents with social, economic, cultural and political goals? Is it to put a powerful idea in parallel with the Ámerican Dream'? Or is it a unique Chinese notion located in Chinese historical conditions? Before we take up these questions, let us see what policy lines have emerged in the early months of Xi Jinping's leadership.

No Policy Shifts?

Though XiJinping's early performance created positive vibrations in China and abroad, it was still not clear what kind of policy choices he was making. Like the generation of Chinese to which he belonged, he seemed to be acutely conscious of the western press and intelligentsia's assessment of each step he took. The economy, culture and the public space in China was so closely interconnected with the West that any Chinese leader had to constantly address both his domestic constituency and the world, in this case, the Western world with which most interest groups in China currently enjoyed shared ventures even though they perceived the US as a competitor in most respects. Yet, on several issues, Xi had directly responded to Chinese people's major concerns soon after being elevated to top leadership. But, his responses and initiatives during the first six months of his assuming office were too cautious or too general to indicate any fresh thinking.

It may be too early to expect new initiatives. But, on crucial issues such as fighting corruption, promoting democracy, carrying forward economic reforms in a desirable direction and on China's global role, the Xi Jinping leadership did not provide adequate clues to its line of action. It also means that he did not wish to make any dramatic break with the policies of the

Hu Jintao regime and may make gradual adjustments to meet the demands of the changing situation. Thus the prediction by some commentators that Xi would veer away from the Hu Jintao line and restore the Jiang Zemin perspective was still not vindicated.[3]

Fighting Corruption

Indeed, Xi has highlighted his anti-corruption drive as a major policy initiative. He not only mentioned it as a principal task in his first meeting with the press on 15 November 2012 and had a special meeting of the Politbureau to chalk out a strategy and guidelines on 4 December, but addressed the full session of the Central Committee on Discipline and Inspection on 23 January. The eight-point guidelines issued by the CPC to improve work style, curb bureaucracy and fight corruption were popularised all over China thereafter. The cases of 73000 officials prosecuted, 4698 punished, 961 handed over to judicial organs in 2012 were reported by the media frequently to show that the party took the anti-corruption drive seriously. A yearlong campaign was launched in April 2013 to clean up the Party by changing four undesirable elements in the work style, namely, formalism, bureaucratism, hedonism and extravagance.

But, as to the approach to fighting corruption, there was still no sign of change. The CPC's Eighteenth Congress Report mentioned "the distinctive Chinese approach to combating corruption and promoting integrity by addressing both its symptoms and root causes, combining punishment and prevention, with emphasis on the latter." In his speech on 17 March 2013 at the conclusion of the 12th National People's Congress Xi Jinping also "pledged to resolutely fight against corruption and other misconduct in all its manifestations and always preserve the political integrity of the of Communists."[4]

What is the prevention strategy that the new leadership has suggested? Like his predecessors Jiang Zemin and Hu Jintao both of whom called corruption as a life-and-death issue for the Party, it is still treated as a 'governance issue' rather than a 'structural issue'. The former approach involves mainly administrative measures by implementing law and regulations while the latter goes to the economic, political and moral dimensions of corruption while subsuming under it the governance aspects. No doubt big fishes have been netted by the anti-corruption drive in the recent period. Xi's statement that his regime would catch both 'tigers and flies' is now a part of the everyday conversation in China. Harsh punishment, executions through summary trials have been meted out. The disgraced Party Secretary of Chongqing, Bo Xilai's indictment on charges of corruption, bribery and abuse of power was announced in July 2013 and his trial was scheduled to commence shortly in Jinan, Shandong Province. In the first few months of the Xi-Li regime a climate of fear among the party cadres had been created lest they were caught for corruption. Xi Jinping has sent out a stern message warning leaders and cadres at every level to abide by rules, be transparent in decision-making and set examples for others.

But, the structural roots of corruption were still not addressed. As long as the growth-centric economic strategy that required high profit by entrepreneurs and managers through a liberalized and, therefore, discretionary regime the scope for corruption would persist. As the Chinese experience as well as that of the other developing countries including India demonstrate such a regime heavily relied upon networks of lobbying and gratification of various kinds, to obtain contracts for manufacture and trade, within the country and abroad, Since the size of the economy and the magnitude of the projects in China is huge, the scale of corruption is also large. It is that kind of economy and its success that has produced an amoral society in contemporary China. Contrast it with the China of yesteryears where socialist values guided people to save and sacrifice for common good rather than accumulate wealth and luxury without limits for personal enjoyment. While it is commendable that governance measures on transparent work style and strict enforcement of law and punishment have been reaffirmed, unless they are accompanied by a set of structural measures changing the obsession with profit-making by any means, and further combined with initiatives to build an environment of moral values, the governance measures by themselves will fail to curb the rising trend of multi-faceted corruption of high magnitude.

This is the lesson from both developed and developing countries.[5] If the realization of the Chinese dream includes providing a clean, corruption-free administration where every citizen enjoys his/her rights under law, then Xi Jinping has to announce a more comprehensive programme to fight corruption. The yearlong clean-up campaign that began in April 2013 which talked of 'self-cultivation' by Party cadres, echoing the message in Liu Shaoqi's famous treatise, "How to be a Good Communist" still did not convey a comprehensive strategy to fight corruption.

Promoting Democracy

Even though the Eighteenth Party Congress clearly ruled out China adopting a Western style democracy, there is still no indication of the kind of democracy that the CPC is trying to evolve. At a theoretical level, Marxists believe that the challenge of a socialist system is to prove that it is more democratic than a capitalist society. Thus far, CPC's one-party rule with multi-party consultation has been explained as necessary for consolidating its path of development within a framework which is sometimes described as 'democracy with Chinese characteristics'. It is seen as having provided political and social stability with which China achieved sustained economic growth. But, the political system has not coped with the steadily rising democratic consciousness among the masses. The protests among workers, farmers, youth and minorities continued to grow. During the first few weeks after Xi assumed the Party leadership, there were fresh cases of clamp down on press and micro blog sites some of which were later relaxed. The 2013 New Years Day Editorial on "Chinese Dream of Constitutionalism" in the Guangzhou journal *Southern Weekend* was censured by the local Party authorities leading to protests by its journalists and local people.

Xi's open invitation for offering criticism while talking to the democratic parties on the eve of the Spring Festival of 2013 conveyed a welcome message. But, there was so much skepticism on this issue that many observers recalled the Anti-

Rightist Campaign of Mao Zedong in 1957. There were many expectations as to whether there would be new initiatives by the new leadership to promote democratic processes. Would Xi Jinping , for example, give a concrete direction to democratic change by raising the level of competitive elections from the Village level to the Xiang and County People's Congress and giving them statutory power of self-governance? A new policy package on Tibet and Xinjiang to provide political autonomy would give a signal that a confident Chinese leadership can walk an extra mile to win the confidence of the minority population and reverse the process of alienation. The incidents of violence in Xinjiang in June 2013 only witnessed more of the same 'strike hard' policies rather than a new policy package of political autonomy, religious freedom, cultural rights and economic development.

However, there was a fresh round of a campaign for 'serve the people' recalling the "putting people first' campaign in the early months of Hu Jintao regime in 2003. It is noteworthy that Xi Jinping has launched a drive to promote 'mass line' reaffirming the need to restore the Party's link with common people. The principle of 'from the masses, to the masses' has once again been a theme of the yearlong campaign to clean up the party.[6] This concept was at the core of Mao Zedong's method of Party-building in the Yanan period, but had not seen prominence in CPC's political work for a long time. Many in the Party feared its connotations having links with the Great Leap Forward and Cultural Revolution. The party's alienation from people is a common refrain of much open discussion in contemporary China. Therefore, the need to change the behavior of cadres has been emphasized as an urgent task by the new leadership. But this trend of alienation has been talked about during the regimes of both Jiang Zemin and Hu Jintao. Under Hu Jintao special measures were initiated under a new governance strategy and the 'scientific outlook of development'. Without taking concrete measures to ensure people's participation in decision-making, the call for 'rejuvenation of the Chinese nation' and realize the Chinese dream may be an abstract notion.

Economic Choices

On the economic front, Xi Jinping is on enormous pressure to resume the high growth path irrespective of its social, political and environmental consequences. Actually, the growth rate of the GDP had picked up once again and crossed 8 per cent in 2012. The goal of doubling the GDP of 2010 by 2020 was achievable. Therefore, the focus had to be on 'changing the growth model' as announced at the Eighteenth Party Congress so that the widening income gap and regional disparity were reversed and the ecological goal of saving resources and reducing pollution was pursued vigorously. In the Politbureau meeting of the CPC in July 2013 the Party decided to stick to the line of pursuing a moderate rate of growth of about seven per cent and change the focus of the growth model as stipulated in the XII Five year Plan. The emphasis on promoting domestic consumption and reducing the dependence on foreign trade was reiterated. It announced the decision to follow a 'human-centric' urbanisation model with focus on raising people's livelihood.[7] This objective was no doubt desirable. But, if that led to catering mainly to the demands of the upper strata in Chinese society and those in the developed coastal region and in mega cities, then, the prevailing social problems would be exacerbated. The new production strategy ought to address the needs of the rural population, tackle the 'three rural problems' of low agricultural productivity, low income of peasants and underdeveloped countryside, meet the demands of the over two hundred million floating population in cities and attend to the growing phenomenon of unemployment. It had to address the problem of environmental degradation even more seriously. The development model had to keep in mind why contemporary China had a rising trend of social unrest. Xi Jinping has inherited a high growth economy which has given substance to his call for pursuing the Chinese dream. But this economic success has come with many contradictions and problems.[8] This had prompted the Hu Jintao leadersip to talk of 'scientific outlook on development' that would be comprehensive and balanced. It is yet to be seen if Xi's Chinese dream concept is indeed fully absorbing the Hu Jintao vision.

China's Global Role

Finally, the emerging global role of China is a point of much debate all over the world today. Having become the second largest world economy in 2010 and continuously gaining high prestige in world scale, China has two sets of options as a global power. One is the path of the earlier big powers, of the colonial era and the post-colonial and post-cold -war era. The US seems to be the model for many of China's foreign policy and security analysts. Just as most Chinese youth aspire to live the American way of life, the policy-makers wish to acquire the economic and military strength to match US power. China's economic success has built up Chinese nationalism along those lines to attain and surpass US. The current discourse on the Chinese dream as a parallel to the discourse on the American dream is naturally seen by many observers as being linked to the great power ambitions of China. The discourse on *Re-Orient* and *Re-emerging Powers* or restoring the glory and dominance of the East in the world reflects that thought. The other is the path of global transformation of the existing hegemonic, unequal, power-governed world into a democratic, equitable, consensus-driven world. China as a permanent member of UN Security Council, a member of G-20 and BRICS can use its privilege either to pursue the big power road or the democratic road.

Soon after assuming the office of the President, Xi Jinping made his first foreign trip to Russia en route to attending the Fifth BRICS Summit in South Africa in March 2013. His Russia visit reaffirmed the close relationship between the two countries. Xi made his participation in the BRICS Summit in Durban as a signature event of his early performance. Before leaving Beijing he met the journalists of the BRICS countries and talked about the priority of protecting the 'legitimate rights and interests of developing countries'.[9] (In this press interaction he also announced his 'five point proposal for improving Sino-Indian ties.) *Dreaming with BRICS* was the theme of much reporting on the Durban Summit in China. Conveying the commitment to changing the unequal world order the Durban Declaration of 27 March 2013 announced: "As the global economy is being reshaped, we are committed to exploring new models and approaches towards more equitable development and inclusive global growth by emphasizing complementarities and building our respective economic strength.[10] However, the issue to examine is whether the BRICS leaders, especially those of China and India wished to follow the same growth model as the Western countries advanced and engage in the same kind of balance of power politics with a new set of big powers managing the world or they would be the agencies for global democratic transformation. At the Boao Forum for Asia in April 2013 Xi underlined the need for reform of the international economic and financial system and called upon Asia to perform its role as the important engine of this transformation for achieving common development. He also said that "the Chinese Dream, namely, the great renewal of the Chinese nation" will be realized and will benefit Asia and the whole world.[11]

It was noteworthy that Chinese Premier Li Keqiang also made his first foreign trip after taking over as Premier, to India in May 2013, and underlined its significance explicitly as a sign of a new stage of understanding between China and India and recognition of a changing world situation where developing countries mattered. Even though there were no notable agreements signed during his visit to India the political significance of his visit was appreciated widely. Equally noteworthy was President Xi Jinping's visit to the Americas in June 2013. He first visited Trinidad and Tobago, Costa Rica and Mexico as if to indicate the precedence contemporary China gave to relations with developing countries. Thereafter Xi Jinping landed in his first visit as President to the US and had a summit meeting with President Obama in Sunnylands, Palm Springs, California on the west coast of the US on 7-8 June 2013 before flying back to Beijing. The informality of the close- door meetings between the two Presidents and their delegations was noted with appreciation in both countries and the summit was billed as the most significant since the Nixon-Mao Summit in 1972. This is where Xi Jinping announced that he would like to evolve 'a new kind of relations between great powers', between an established power and an emerging power.[12] There were no doubt many issues of conflict in their foreign, economic and strategic policies, but there is an apprehension that both sides seemed to perceive themselves as the Group of Two (G 2) to manage the world's big problems. Would China be a relatively status quoist power maintain the prevailing strategic balance in Asia and the world and the trade and finance system both of which had facilitated its economic growth as the second largest world economy in the recent decades? The cyber security issues, de-nuclearization of the Korean Peninsula , the large trade deficit of US with China were some of the critical issues taken up during the summit. But Obama's statement that China's rise as a great power was good for US and the world was a much quoted expression giving rise to the concrete emergence of a new US-China framework in world scale. The discussion on the Chinese Dream picked up momentum in the US press and comparisons and contrasts were made. One Senator called it a nightmare if China achieved its dream of becoming a world power and functioned as a global hegemon.[13]

Thus Xi Jinping's much publicised talk of the Chinese dream and the stress on the agenda of rejuvenation of the Chinese nation and its five thousand year old civilization can work either way. It can be translated into the agenda of becoming a dominant world power. On the other hand, the 'peaceful rise of China' can also be a civilizational catalyst for transforming the unequal world. However, the Chinese leaders can certainly draw lessons from history. The 21st century clearly marks the surging wave of self-determination of people and nations in all parts of the world against all forms of hegemony and that cannot be missed by modern rulers of any country.

At the end of the first half-year of his leadership it had become clear that Xi Jinping did not wish to be identified with the political line or leadership style of either Hu Jintao or Jiang Zemin. He would perhaps eventually fashion his own mode of leadership. It was expected by many within China and abroad that in the coming days, Xi would make clear choices on how to fight corruption in a comprehensive way, promote democracy more confidently through institutional innovations, orient development towards equity, sustainability and build China as a democratic force for global peace and equity. The future performance on those issues would clarify the meaning of the Chinese dream.

What is the Chinese Dream?

First of all, it should be mentioned that Xi Jinping did not initiate the discourse on the Chinese Dream; he picked it up, saying that "it was a hot topic at present", and made it a national slogan of the Party and the state. Even the claim that the *New York Times* journalist Thomas Friedman coined the term is not quite accurate even though it became a significant reference in the media. He also joined an already unfolding discussion in the recent years, even though his article did get special attention in China. Leading up to the Eighteenth Party Congress, Friedman wrote in one of his articles, entitled, "China needs its own Dream"—a dream that 'marries people's expectations of prosperity with a more sustainable China". He further said: "Because the next government's dream for China's emerging middle class-300 million people expected to grow to 800 million by 2025—is just like the American Dream (a big car, a big house, McDonald's Big mac for all) then we need another planet."[14] He also referred to the "Chinese Dream Project" of Peggy Liu, and also to the environment NGO, JUCCCE. In fact, there were books and articles even before. Li Junru of the Central Party School had published in 2006, *The China Dream: China in Peaceful Development* which became a popular point of reference.[15] Until then the focus of this discourse in China was on achieving success in course of the economic reforms and assuring the world that China's rise was peaceful and did not pose any threat to others. The tenor of this debate changed with the publication in 2010, *The China Dream: Great Power Thinking and Strategic Posture in the Post-American Era* by Col. Liu Mingfu of National Defense University. This was the most discussed book since its publication and it had a clear message. Liu wanted to see China as world's number one military power and with comprehensive economic strength to back it.[16]

In the West there were other publications as well. A 2003 book by a business journalist uses the term in a very different vein warning the western investors of the pitfalls of their "China dream" of excessive interest in the China market which faced many uncertainties. On the other hand, Helen Wang, a Chinese student who stayed on in US wrote *The Chinese Dream: The Rise of the World's Largest Middle Class and What it Means to You* (2010) which portrayed the spectacular economic growth in China and the enormous opportunities it offered the world; while wondering at the same time if China was following the western path of development or had abiding links with the Chinese civilization.[17] A critical account of the consequences of the pattern of growth was given by Gerard Lemos in his 2012 book, *The End of the Chinese Dream: Why Chinese People Fear the Future* where he chronicles the numerous social and health problems that the people of Chongqing face in their daily life.[18]

But Xi Jinping steered this discussion in a distinctly different direction to inspire the people of China to work for a historic mission that the CPC had put before them. Even then the meaning and dimensions of the Chinese dream discourse remained manifold.

A Framework for Mobilization

The theoretical journal of the Party, *Qiushi (Seeking Truth)* in its 1 May 2013 Editorial gave an authoritative introduction to the discourse on the Chinese dream. It was entitled, *The Chinese Dream: Infuses Socialism with Chinese Characteristics with New Energy*. Referring to the 5000 years of history of China and the antecedents of such formulation in the modern period it referred to *Grand Harmony* (*da tong*) of Kang Youwei and the constitutionalism initiatives of Liang Qichao, the reformers of the early twentieth century, Dr Sun Yatsen's leadership of the Xinhai Revolution of 1911 and the slogans of 'science and democracy' in the May Fourth Movement each of which embodied elements of the Chinese dream. It said that only the CPC's leadership of the Chinese revolution and the building of socialism with Chinese characteristics had taken the right steps to realize these aspirations. The Editorial then proceeded to identify eight tasks announced at the 18th Party Congress as the very dimensions of the programme to realize the Chinese dream:

> ...persist in the dominant role of the people, persist in liberating and developing social productive forces, persist in moving reform and opening up forward, persist in safeguarding social justice and fairness, persist in marching on the path of common prosperity, persist in stimulating social harmony, persist in peaceful development, and persist in the leadership of the Party.

Of the above items three have attracted a great deal of attention in the Chinese public discourse. First, the prosperity of each individual is as important as that of the entire nation. So macro-development is not given precedence over micro-development. Hu Jintao's reformulation of the 2020 goal as establishing a 'well-off society in all respects' and achieving doubling of the per capita income both for urban and rural people are relevant here.[19] Secondly, Social inequality is addressed by the accent on social justice and fairness keeping in view the problem of expanding social unrest in several sections of society. Thirdly, there is a message for the world to assure people outside China that Chinese dream is to work for a 'harmonious world' and it did not pose any threat to neighbours or other powers. Reportedly, Xi Jinping said as much to President Obama at their summit in Sunnylands.

However, western commentators are not convinced about the official Chinese interpretations. *The Economist* noticed in it a 'calculated opacity' to create a climate for nationalist appeal.[20] An Op-Ed article in *The New York Times* argued that Xi Jinping's Chinese Dream could be a stimulus for greater reforms or it could be a cause for fear making him "a nationalist who set China on an aggressive course of bullying its neighbours and confronting US."[21]

It is interesting that the Chinese commentators have been at pains to differentiate the Chinese dream from the American dream as much as the Americans have. Those believing in the American dream claim that irrespective of social origins of class, race and place of birth every American can achieve full realization of his/her potentiality through the equality of opportunity provided in that society. In other words, anyone who works hard can get a fair chance to lead a happy life in the United States of America. This assumption has been frequently contested in the US itself saying that still the blacks and poor migrants and women are structurally discriminated against and inequalities have grown in unprecedented scale in the recent decades.[22] The struggle for social, economic, cultural and political equality especially in terms of race, gender and class still goes on in the US. One Chinese theoretician focuses on the Chinese historical conditions warranting a national renewal to point out the difference.[23] Indeed the nineteenth century clamour for a 'rich people and strong nation' (*Fumin qiang guo*) is very much part of the new assertion in China. They are included in Xi Jinping's 17 March address to the NPC which called for building a 'rich, strong, democratic, civilized, harmonious socialist country' Each of these terms needed qualification. For example, being rich also was to be accompanied by being sustainable. Democratic did not mean following the Western model.

A ' nation without a dream is a nation without a hope', said one commentator in China, 'Having a dream bring people the motivation to work hard, accept challenges and promote change... for better education, stable jobs, higher incomes, greater social security, better medical and healthcare, improved housing conditions, better environmental quality'.[24] Thus it can be reduced to being general mobilization framework to fulfil the usual aspirations of people in every country. But as a scholar put it, "the Chinese dream is not the same for all Chinese, China is very complex, I do not see any paradigm shift and I am not sure if the rhetoric is going to last."[25]

This slogan can indeed be a mobilizational strategy of the new leadership to consolidate its political base and strengthen its appeal. Jiang Zemin's Three Represents did not attract the same kind of emotional appeal and it was announced towards the fag end of his tenure. Hu Jintao's Scientific Development Outlook may have been an important intervention to reorient China's growth strategy, though with little success, but it did not touch the deep sentiments of a nationalist Chinese. During his tenure the Beijing Olympics logo 'One world One Dream' symbolized his notion of the 'harmonious world'. For Xi Jinping who faces many serious challenges in Chinese society and the world, there was perhaps a need for a new mantra of mobilization even without making any obvious break with the existing policies. Yet his call for moving with the times gives him all the flexibility he needs to innovate and launch new policies. As he put it:

> We must make persistent efforts to press ahead with indomitable will, continue to push forward the great cause of socialism with Chinese characteristics, and strive to achieve the Chinese dream of great rejuvenation of the Chinese nation.... To realize the Chinese road, we must spread the Chinese spirit, which combines the spirit of the Chinese nation with patriotism as the core and the spirit of the time with reform and innovation as the core.[26]

Decisions at the Third Plenum of November 2013

To put some concrete form to the call for realising the Chinese Dream Xi Jinping led the CPC Central Committee to adopt a sixty-point decision at its Third Plenum held on 9-12 November 2013. It took a few significant decisions which were publicised in China and abroad as momentous, claimed to be comparable to the Third Plenum of 1978 which had inaugurated China's reform path under Deng Xiaoping's leadership. But in reality they carried forward the trends started during the Hu Jintao regime, no doubt with greater emphasis. Firstly, the market forces were to play now a 'decisive' role whereas until now they were playing a 'basic' or 'fundamental' role. Interest rates and prices were to be determined more directly by the market. This may indicate that the Jiang Zemin line was more powerful now. But the state was still to continue to play the key role in maintaining economic stability, provide public services, and guarantee fair competition and so on. Therefore the practice will clarify the new decision further. The second measure was to reform the SOEs (State Owned Enterprises)—a process that has gone on for over a decade and has been a major part of China's twelfth five year plan. The SOEs are asked to contribute not 15 per cent as now, but 30 per cent of their profit to the national exchequer. For that they have to undergo more reorganization. Third, the rural land policy and migration policy will be liberalized further. The farmers who now cultivate land under household responsibility system will be allowed to mortgage their land and sell their home directly even though the overall policy of the village collective owning the village land will continue. However the picture will be clearer when the rules are worked out in the near future. The *Hukou* (household registration system) system has been increasingly relaxed during the past two decades allowing rural residents to go to towns and cities to work. Even though in the big cities they are not entitled to the education, health and welfare benefits, in many small and intermediate towns they are already availing such benefits. This process will be expanded as this unfair practice of denying the migrant workers their legitimate benefits has been a big source of discontent in present-day China.

The other measures which are likely to gain popularity for the Xi Jinping leadership are the change in the one child policy and abolition of the 'detention in labour camps'. The one child policy in force since 1980 may have succeeded in keeping China's population explosion in check, but it has created many structural problems. China is fast becoming an ageing society. The son preference in rural China has made the prospects of the girl child precarious. The exceptions which had already emerged in many cases are now a matter of policy. If both the parents are single child of their parents they can go for having two children now. The other, the labour camp phenomenon has been in existence from the days of the Cultural Revolution. Instead of putting people in prisons the Chinese government put most of them, especially the political prisoners, in rural areas to do manual labour and undergo reform. Human rights bodies had challenged such forms of punishment and now this system stands abolished. In addition to these, Xi has announced greater independence for the judiciary and more freedom for the 'social organisations' or NGOs—measures which are likely to contribute to the building of his image of being seriously committed to rule of law. But incidents of suppression of dissidents and occasional blocking of the internet continue to occur even though there is a general feeling of relaxation of the political environment in contemporary China. The Plenum has also decided to set up a "National Security Council' with President Xi as the head to coordinate the security functions domestic and international. It was also decided to set up a "Core Group of the Party to Steer the Reforms" showing determination to address the set of issues ranging from the rate growth to equity and sustainability and global financial situation.

Indeed these are important decisions relating to institutional changes and policy directions. But how they are implemented in the next few years will indicate whether Xi Jinping is in the process of evolving a fresh perspective to steer China ahead to realise the Chinese Dream.

Globally there have been two kinds of discourses on dreams. One kind of articulation is associated with writers, philosophers, leaders of social movements, revolutions and political struggles. Mahatma Gandhi, for example, has written about "India of my dream". Bhagat Singh, the revolutionary leader too had a powerful statement on his vision of India. Martin Luther King's 1963 speech in Washington DC, "I have a dream", remains an ever inspiring milestone for the movements, not only in the US but all over the world, for social and political equality and dignity for all. These are attributed to particular leaders who were visionaries and therefore provided inspirations for succeeding generations. The earlier Chinese articulations of the visions of future of China by Liang Qichao, Sun Yatsen, Lu Xun and Mao Zedong were of the same order. Another kind of articulation is to characterize it as a national dream and propagate it as such. The American dream and the recent articulation of the Chinese dream are of that order. They are bound to b problematized, contested and rearticulated from various vantage points from time to time.

But it is good to have dreams. As the people's poet Paas said, "you may forget everything and it may still be possible to recover them, but *sabse khatarnaakh hai apne sapno ko bhul jana* (It is most dangerous to forget one's dreams). But what kind of dream one has is important to ascertain. Xi Jinping has an arduous task of proving in practice what he means by the Chinese dream unless it is only his mode of mobilization of the Chinese people.

NOTES

1. *Xinhuanet* (English), 29 November 2012.
2. Xi Stresses adherence to socialism, serving the people', *Xinhua, People's Daily Online*, 26 June 2013.
3. This speculation was rife at the time of the Eighteenth Party Congress. See Manoranjan Mohanty, 'Harmonious Society': Hu Jintao's Vision and the Chinese Party Congress, *The Economic and Political Weekly*, Vol. XLVII, No. 50 (15 December 2012).
4. President Xi Pledges Resolute Fight against Corruption, *Xinhua* (English), 17 March 2013.
5. For a discussion on a major anti-corruption campaign in India see ManoranjanMohanty, "People's Movements and the Anna Upsurge", *The Economic and Political Weekly*, Vol. XLVI, No. 38 (2011), pp. 16-9.
6. Meng Na, Mass Line Campaign Key to Consolidate CPC's Ruling Status, Xinhua, *People's Daily Online* (19 June 2013).
7. CPC Leadership decides to keep China's economic growth stable, *Xinhua* (31 July 2013).
8. Manoranjan Mohanty, China's Success Trap: Lessons for Development Theory. MIDS Founder's Day Lecture (Chennai: Madras Institute of Development Studies, 18 April 2013).
9. *Indian Express* (New Delhi, 19 March 2013).
10. "Durban Declaration and Action Plan (27 March 2013) in www.brics5.co.za
11. Xi Jinping's address at Boao Forum for Asia on 7 April 2013 did however did commit China to 'narrowing north-south gap' and 'reform of the international economy.' News.xinhuanet.com/ English/china/2013-04-07/C.
12. Obama-Xi try to avoid Cold War Mentality', *New York Times* (9 June 2013).
13. Marco Rubio, "Do Two Dreams Equal a Nightmare?" Foreign Policy (foreignpolicy.com: 7 June 2013)
14. Thomas Friedman, "China needs its own Dream", *New York Times* (2 October 2012).
15. Li Junru, The China Dream: China in Peaceful Development (Beijing: Foreign Languages Press, 2006) In 2012 Li was Vice-President of China Reform Forum, an influential advisory group of the Party.
16. Liu Mingfu, *Zhongguo Meng: Hou meiguo shidai de daguo siwei zhanlue dingwei* (Beijing: Zhongguo youyi chuban gongsi, 2010) for a summary see Christopher R Hughes, *The China Beat* (5 April 2010).

17. Helen Wang, *The Chinese Dream: The Rise of the World's Largest Middle Class and What it Means to You*. (New York: Create Space Independent Publishing, 2010).
18. Gerard Lemos, *The End of the Chinese Dream: Why Chinese People Fear the Future* (New Haven, Conn.: Yale University Press, 2012).
19. China Dream concerns happiness of all Chinese individuals and the nation as a whole, *China Daily* (27 June 2013).
20. Chasing the Chinese Dream, *The Economist* (4 May 2013).
21. Robert L Kuhn, Xi Jinping's Chinese Dream, *The New York Times* (4 June 2013).
22. How this is an ambiguous and elastic concept is shown by Jim Cullen, *The American Dream: A Short History of an Idea that Shaped a Nation* (New York: Oxford University Press, 2004). How extent and dimensions of inequality have been accentuated in the US in the recent years is shown by Joseph Stiglitz in *The Price of Ineuality* (New York: W W Norton and Norton, 2012).
23. Shi Yuzhi, Seven Reasons why the Chinese Dream is different from the American Dream, Qiushi (20 May 2013)
24. Guo Fenghai quoted in *China Daily* (27 June 2013)
25. A Peking University Economist quoted in *China Daily* (27 June 2013)
26. Xi Jin Ping's address to the concluding session of NPC, *Xihua* (English) (17 March 2013).

Conclusion

CPC's Ideology: Some Reflections

A Methodology of Assessment

There are two approaches to assessing the performance of self-proclaimed communist parties. One is to apply the criteria that one considers to be the original tenets of Marxism. Here too there are choices to be made because there would be many different interpretations of what those original tenets are.[1] Then there is the other approach that allows the practicing communist party or leadership or philosopher a creative development of Marxism, applying the original tenets to the changed conditions, in particular the geographical and the historical situation that they confront. The second approach takes their formulations for serious consideration and assessment.

It is the latter approach that has stood the test of time. All communist parties, from Lenin's time onwards have made fresh formulations using original ideas of Marx and Engels. But on each occasion of such reformulation, there have been dissenting voices and often splits in the communist movement. The literature on Marxism is rich and abundant on the history of these debates. The Stalin-Trotsky debate had set the broad pattern of these ideological debates and organizational splits. The critics of a certain line would call that line either 'left adventurist' or 'right revisionist' depending on their respective vantage points. Sometimes these debates took place within a communist party and it was called the inner-party struggle. In most cases it led to splits giving rise to new parties or formations as evident in contemporary India.

This is not the place to go into the history of Marxism or communist movement. I only wish to identify the vantage point from where I present an assessment of the CPC ideology.[2] My vantage point is what I call socialism in the twenty first century. It is not in the sense the late Hugo Chavez used the term, not even entirely echoing the Nepalese Maoists' formulation using this phrase, but very much sharing their cumulative ideas as well as issues from recent history of the world. Taking the challenge of global capitalism in its twenty first century form as the principal task for socialist revolution, and therefore pursuing class politics as the central task, the new socialists take all forms of social contradictions seriously, such as gender, caste, race, religion, age. This is because workers are male or female, from upper or lower caste, majority or minority religion and so on. Together with class and social contradictions, the environmental dimension of economic development is central to the notion of human liberation that was the key concern of Marxism as the rise of capitalism has turned out to be a catastrophe for natural resources and environment. For all this, building of a new culture of human civilization that was for promotion of this process of liberation was necessary. Hence the notion of relative autonomy of culture in its relationship with material forces is built into the method of dialectical and historical materialism. The pursuit of liberation from class, caste, gender, religion in life experience also meant exercise of power by the oppressed classes in concrete institutional practice. Thus practice of democracy and realization of human rights are today integral to contemporary struggle for socialism.Therefore, socialism as 'development of productive forces' that was directed to the goal of equality at one level in the stage of socialism—each according to his/her capacity- each according to his/her work- and at another level in the stage of communism —each according to his/her need—has now meant this process of human emancipation in the twenty first century. This is how the 'dialectics of dialectical and historical materialism' had unfolded thus far and will further unfold in yet uncharted dimensions.[3]

My study of the Chinese Revolution taught me the meaning of the method of creative development of Marxism to adapt to changing historical conditions. Accordingly I formulated the notion of 'revolutionary strategy' as a dialectical synthesis of ideology and environment pursued by a revolutionary organization.[4]If it was derived only from ideology then it was likely to be dogmatic and may fail to overcome the challenges of the environment. If it was merely a response to immediate environment it would be opportunistic and pragmatic not moving in the direction of cherished goals.

But whether all changed formulations are theoretical acts of revolutionary creativity is a matter of debate. Mao Zedong's theory of new-democratic revolution that successfully brought into being the PRC and inspired revolutions all over the third world was no doubt one of cases of creative application of Marxism. Yet even this is contested by followers of Trotsky.

In the essay on *Mao's Portrait of Stalin* in this volume, I use this method and show how Mao made a discriminating evaluation of Stalin by pointing out the areas where he was wrong while adoring his contribution. In the chapter on *Power of History: Mao Zedong Thought in Deng's China* I point out the way Deng Xiaoping assessed the role of Mao and his thought and set the theoretical line for his successors. Hu Jintao's speech at the CPC's ninetieth anniversary in 2011 reflected the same approach. Such interpretations of earlier leaders, especially Mao, also had political consequences such as getting legitimacy in the eyes of masses while breaking sharply with Mao's policies.

We will follow the method of 'dialectics of dialectical and historical materialism' and make a brief assessment of the formulations of the reform period and the course of evolution of CPC's ideology. Our criteria of assessment will be whether CPC's ideological evolution stood the tests of socialism in the twenty first century.

Socialism with Chinese Characteristics

China's reforms since 1978 were theorized by Deng Xiaoping as 'building socialism with Chinese characteristics' which forms the theme of many of the chapters of this volume. Promoting market economy under state control is the main characteristic of China's 'socialist market economy'. Deng Xiaoping and his successors asserted that it was a historical innovation in China since such an experiment had not taken place so far in human history. And the Chinese reform policy started with trials of market experiments in some sectors and in some areas in China, which were generalized as national policy later. The theoretical statement came much later in 1992 at the Fourteenth Congress of the CPC.

As we have seen before it all started with the policy of 'reform and open door'. To put it in simple terms, reform meant making all enterprises responsive to markets and open door meant inviting capital from within the country and from abroad to invest. That process infused new momentum into the Chinese economy and economic growth surged into new heights making China world's second largest economy in 2010.

It was a new model of development. But was it a socialist model? The oft-quoted saying of Deng Xiaoping that 'it did not matter whether the cat was black or white if it caught mice' was in defence of the merits of market economy. According to him market economy had no class character it was 'a feature of the modern age' like technology and management.

Three decades of market economy in China, despite state control, has produced a capitalist class. Jiang Zemin's 'important thought of Three Represents' was actually meant to legitimize the emergent bourgeoisie in China and opened the door to them for membership of the CPC. In addition to representing advanced productive forces and advanced culture (science and technology) the Party was called upon to represent the interest of the broad masses which was interpreted as the entrepreneurs and managers.

The preoccupation with economic growth and creation of urban infrastructure of the kind that exist in metropolises of the western countries was so paramount that it defined China's nationalist aspirations and seemed to fulfill them. Rise of China became the talk of the globe. Theoreticians in CPC came up with formulations such as 'peaceful rise of China' and 'peaceful development of China'.[5]

The average Chinese citizen experienced greatly enhanced standard of living during these years. The magnitude of poverty was reduced considerably. China's prestige in the world rose to new heights. But at the same time social disparities grew enormously. Once one of the world's least unequal society became one of world's most unequal society (gini coefficient 1982: 0.30 but 2008 : 0.49) rivaling US and beating India. Regional disparities expanded beyond expectations despite the Western Development Strategy. China became the world's number one emitter of carbon dioxide in 2011. Environmental destruction was so acute that it became one of the major objectives of the XI and XII five year plans to curb pollution. Corruption in general and particularly in high places continued to rise despite many stringent measures. I have analysed China's success story as a Success Trap elsewhere.[6]

It is to address these problems that Hu Jintao formulated his 'Scientific Outlook of Development' which was to be comprehensive, balanced and coordinated development. He outlined the CPC mission as achieving a fivefold goal of social, political, economic, cultural and ecological development. Building a 'harmonious society' that responded to all social contradictions and a 'beautiful country' that was ecologically sustainablewas the declaration at the Eighteenth Party Congress.

Deng Xiaoping had set the course of China's development as a market economy. Jiang Zemin vigorously pursued that programme giving full play to capitalist initiatives. Hu Jintao strode on the same path, but trying to tackle the problems that had arisen along the way. His efforts failed to achieve a course correction even though he put on record the need to achieve a 'pattern transformation' and 'change in the growth model'. The structural logic of market economy that created the social base of capitalism in "China was so strong that Hu Jintao's effort could hardly alter that characteristic.

Xi Jinping has inherited that China. He has invoked the five thousand year old civilisational identity of China, reminded the humiliation it had suffered for almost two centuries in the hands of colonialism and put before the Chinese people a slogan of realising the 'Chinese dream of national rejuvenation'. His early performance has aroused hopes of greater concern for equity, justice and sustainability, clean and responsive governance and addressing day-to-day problems faced by people of China. But it is still not clear whether he has some fresh ideas for achieving those objectives.

Interestingly, he has invoked the spirit of communism and called upon Party members to cultivate communist values of service to people and mass line. But whether it is mainly a mode of legitimation or more than that only the future will tell.

Détente Social Science in the Age of Globalisation

The Chinese Academy Social Sciences (CASS) invited research projects on Chinese dream in early 2013. It will certainly produce copious volumes on this new subject that would popularize the slogan on the Chinese Dream. This exercise continues a stream of social science development in China that started in a major way in the 1980s which I have discussed in one of the chapters.

Since market economy linked the US society with the Chinese society the academic and intellectual integration continued to grow in leaps and bounds. Deng Xiaoping gave the call to 'seek truth from facts' (*shishiqiushi*) to show that the Maoist policies in practice did not yield results such as higher growth and better living standards. He also empowered the CASS with major investment to study in detail the socio-economic processes. Unlike in India the CASS functioned as a major component of policy-making and knowledge input in China. Though different in form it was comparable to the social science inputs from think tanks and university researches into US policy-making.

To acquire foreign technology and knowledge and reduce the gap with the US, the Chinese knowledge institutions both in social and natural sciences teamed up with US and other western institutions and universities. Every important book published in the west was translated into Chinese and nearly every Department in Chinese Universities had a collaboration arrangement with a western university. Many Chinese students trained in US settled in US and many of them worked in both countries. Many US scholars had joint appointment in US and

China. Media and publication industry and finally the information industry integrated China with the US and other western countries.

Détente social science or the social science of the global capitalist era became the main source of knowledge and understanding in China.

Is Contemporary China a Socialist Society?

At the end of over three decades of reforms how far has the Chinese society moved in the direction of socialism? The answer to this question depends on one's definition of socialism. Keeping in view the notion of socialism that underlies the discussion in this volume, the answer is that today's China is a fast developing capitalist society with many unique features, one of which is that it is ruled by a Communist Party. Much of the new policies were launched in the name of handling contradictions during the early stage of socialism. The assumption was that it was going to be a long period of transformation, as we analysed in this volume. But the trends of the past three decades show the strengthening of the structural logic that fosters a new bourgeoisie, new values of capitalism, power structures that sustain them and firm linkages with global capitalist system. But the debate on these trends of development in China, the nature of their successes and failures still go on in China.

Deng's critique of Mao, as we have discussed in this volume, was that socialism was not about poverty. That line of thinking triggered a fast pace of growth of China resulting in the quadrupling of China's per capita income between 1980 and 2000 as chalked out by Deng and its further doubling by 2010. It is poised to double again by 2020. The focus on the growth of production made China the world's second largest economy in 2010 surpassing Japan. In 2040 if not earlier China is predicted to beat the US to become the largest economy of the world. The face of urban China transformed so much that it resembled metropolitan centres of developed western countries.

The question is whether socialism is about higher incomes alone. During the decade of Hu Jintao leadership this was debated in China and as we have seen, Hu did not succeed very much in reorienting this strategy towards equity, social justice and environmental sustainability. But he recorded the attempt in that direction reviving socialist objectives and his 'scientific outlook on development', though not framed ideologically in classical Marxist terms, did address the qualitative issues of socialism. He redefined the goal for 2020 as 'well off society in all respects' and aimed at doubling both rural and urban per capita income.

Xi Jinping had not shown signs of fully abandoning the Hu Jintao line as of the autumn of 2013. In fact, the decision to limit the growth rate to 7 or 7.5—which is quite high on world standards, but not in double digits as was the push during the past decade is a pointer. His emphasis on 'self-cultivation' of the communist cadres and the steps to address corruption, abuse of power, indulgence in luxury are also noteworthy. It indicates his sensitivity to the ideological degeneration that the party organization has seen with its total preoccupation to show high growth performance at every level. Xi has stressed that the cadre's popularity among people and his/her ability to solve their concrete problems and their clean record are more important for promotion than showing economic growth performance. Thus the discourse on the Chinese dream which has become the trademark of Xi, which is yet another formulation not flowing directly from familiar Marxist lexicon, is being used to address some of the serious problems resulting from 'growth-centric' reforms. As we have seen these were identified clearly at the Eighteenth Party Congress in November 2012 and Xi Jinping's leadership will be judged in the near future on the successes he was able to achieve in tackling these problems.

Socialism in the Twenty First Century

It is noteworthy that every CPC leader has emphasized the need to 'creatively apply Marxism' to the Chinese conditions and respond adequately to the changed circumstances. Mao Zedong's 'people's democratic revolution', Deng Xiaoping's 'socialism with Chinese characteristics', Jiang Zemin's 'Three

Represents', Hu Jintao's 'Scientific Outlook of Development' were all advanced from that perspective and were mentioned in that vein in the Party constitution that was amended accordingly on every occasion. Xi Jinping too has stressed it in the June 2013 Politbureau deliberations. But it is clear that the dialectics of the evolving contradictions in the twenty first century are still not adequately handled by the CPC leadership.

The new contradictions relate to the civilisational crisis of the capitalist epoch and the democratic practice of an era when people demand political, economic, social and cultural rights. The CPC seems to have fully adopted the cosmology of the capitalist epoch that produces high energy, high speed, high rise, high consumption which is based on achieving high growth of production. This outlook has generated more and more inequalities and injustices in societies and regions as well as new vulnerabilities to natural hazards across the globe. Such a development path is environmentally unsustainable. The awareness about the limits of this model is growing all over the world including China, but the measures taken in response are only marginal while the dominant growth model persists. The other sphere is democracy and self-development in a multidimensional way. Individuals and oppressed groups, classes, races, men and women, religious groups, castes and all regions want to make their own destiny and seek liberation from multiple dominations. And no amount of economic development alone can sufficiently respond to the urges of self-realisation. It should be noted that formal structures of participation and self-governance, not supported by economic, social and cultural guarantees for autonomy, would not suffice as empowerment. This is why Chinese policies in Tibet and Xinjiang and India's policies in Kashmir and Northeast have not satisfied local people's urges for selfhood.

A new cosmology at the end of the exhaustion of the capitalist epoch and a new concept of democracy today anchor the emerging perspective on socialism in the twentieth century. The CPC ideology seems to be still at bay on these new challenges.

NOTES

1. I have tried one such articulation in my essay on"Marxism and Neo-Marxism" in the entry in *Encyclopedia of Global Studies* (Los Angeles: Sage, 2012).
2. My first essay on this subject where I formulated a preliminary method of assessment was "Erosion and Explosion in Marxist Theory", *China Report*, Vol. 9 No. 1 (January 1973) pp. 32-8.
3. I discussed this in "Socialism Tomorrow", *Frontier*, March 21, 1991.
4. Manoranjan Mohanty, *Revolutionary Violence : A Study of the Maoist Movement in India* (New Delhi: Sterling, 1977).
5. Zheng Bijian, *Peaceful Rise of China: Speeches of Zheng Bijian 1997-2004* (Washington D.C.: The Brookings Institution, 2005).
6. For an account of these trends see Manoranjan Mohanty, "China's Success Trap: Lessons in Development Theory", MIDS Founder's Day Lecture 2013 (Chennai: Madras Institute of Development Studies, 2013).

Appendix

Constitution of the Communist Party of China 2012 : The General Program

The Communist Party of China is the vanguard both of the Chinese working class and of the Chinese people and the Chinese nation. It is the core of leadership for the cause of socialism with Chinese characteristics and represents the development trend of China's advanced productive forces, the orientation of China's advanced culture and the fundamental interests of the overwhelming majority of the Chinese people. The realization of communism is the highest ideal and ultimate goal of the Party.

The Communist Party of China takes Marxism-Leninism, Mao Zedong Thought, Deng Xiaoping Theory, the important thought of Three Represents and the Scientific Outlook on Development as its guide to action.

Marxism-Leninism brings to light the laws governing the development of the history of human society. Its basic tenets are correct and have tremendous vitality. The highest ideal of communism pursued by the Chinese Communists can be realized only when the socialist society is fully developed and highly advanced. The development and improvement of the socialist system is a long historical process. So long as the Chinese Communists uphold the basic tenets of Marxism-Leninism and follow the road suited to China's specific conditions and chosen by the Chinese people of their own accord, the socialist cause in China will be crowned with final victory.

The Chinese Communists, with Comrade Mao Zedong as their chief representative, created **Mao Zedong Thought** by integrating the basic tenets of Marxism-Leninism with the concrete practice of the Chinese revolution. Mao Zedong Thought is Marxism-Leninism applied and developed in China; it consists of a body of theoretical principles concerning the revolution and construction in China and a summary of experience therein, both of which have been proved correct by practice; and it represents the crystallized, collective wisdom of the Communist Party of China. Under the guidance of Mao Zedong Thought, the Communist Party of China led the people of all ethnic groups in the country in their prolonged revolutionary struggle against imperialism, feudalism and bureaucrat-capitalism, winning victory in the new-democratic revolution and founding the People's Republic of China, a people's democratic dictatorship. After the founding of the People's Republic, it led them in carrying out socialist transformation successfully, completing the transition from New Democracy to socialism, establishing the basic system of socialism and developing socialism economically, politically and culturally.

After the Third Plenary Session of the Eleventh Party Central Committee, the Chinese Communists, with **Comrade Deng Xiaoping as their chief representative,** analyzed their experience, both positive and negative, gained since the founding of the People's Republic, emancipated their minds, sought truth from facts, shifted the focus of the work of the whole Party onto economic development and carried out reform and opening to the outside world, ushering in a new era of development in the cause of socialism, gradually formulating the line, principles and policies concerning the building of socialism with Chinese characteristics and expounding the basic questions concerning the building, consolidation and development of socialism in China, and thus creating Deng Xiaoping Theory. **Deng Xiaoping Theory** is the outcome of the integration of the basic tenets of Marxism-Leninism with the practice of contemporary China and the features of the times, a continuation and development of Mao Zedong Thought under new historical conditions; it represents a new stage of development of Marxism in China, it is Marxism of contemporary China and it is the crystallized, collective wisdom of the Communist Party of China. It is guiding the socialist modernization of China from victory to victory.

After the Fourth Plenary Session of the Thirteenth Party Central Committee and in the practice of building socialism with Chinese characteristics, the Chinese Communists, with **Comrade Jiang Zemin as their chief representative,** acquired a deeper understanding of what socialism is, how to build it and what kind of party to build and how to build it, accumulated new valuable experience in running the Party and state and formed **the important thought of Three Represents**. The important thought of Three Represents is a continuation and development of Marxism-Leninism, Mao Zedong Thought and Deng Xiaoping Theory; it reflects new requirements for the work of the Party and state arising from the developments and changes in China and other parts of the world today; it serves as a powerful theoretical weapon for strengthening and improving Party building and for promoting self-improvement and development of socialism in China; and it is the crystallized, collective wisdom of the Communist Party of China. It is a guiding ideology that the Party must uphold for a long time to come. Persistent implementation of the Three Represents is the foundation for building the Party, the cornerstone for its governance and the source of its strength.

Since the Party's Sixteenth National Congress, the Chinese Communists with **Comrade Hu Jintao as their chief representative**, following the guidance of Deng Xiaoping Theory and the important thought of Three Represents, have gained a deep understanding of major questions such as what kind of development China should achieve under new conditions and how it should achieve it to meet new requirements for development and answered these questions, and thus developed **the Scientific Outlook on Development** that puts people first and calls for comprehensive, balanced and sustainable development. The Scientific Outlook on Development is a scientific theory that is both in keeping with

Marxism-Leninism, Mao Zedong Thought, Deng Xiaoping Theory and the important thought of Three Represents and is in step with the times. It fully embodies the Marxist worldview on and methodology for development and represents the latest achievement in adapting Marxism to China's conditions. It is the crystallization of the collective wisdom of the Communist Party of China and a guiding ideology that must be upheld and applied in developing socialism with Chinese characteristics.

The fundamental reason behind all of China's achievements and progress since the reform and opening up policy was introduced is, in the final analysis, that the Party has blazed a path of socialism with Chinese characteristics, formulated the **system of theories of socialism with Chinese characteristics,** and established the socialist system with Chinese characteristics. All Party members must cherish the path, the theories and the socialist system that the Party has explored and created after going through all the hardships; and they must keep to them all the time and continue to develop them. They must hold high the great banner of socialism with Chinese characteristics and strive to fulfill the three historic tasks of advancing the modernization drive, achieving national reunification, and safeguarding world peace and promoting common development.

China is in the primary stage of socialism and will remain so for a long time to come. This is a historical stage which cannot be skipped in socialist modernization in China which is backward economically and culturally. It will last for over a hundred years. In socialist construction the Party must proceed from China's specific conditions and take the path of socialism with Chinese characteristics. At the present stage, the principal contradiction in Chinese society is one between the ever-growing material and cultural needs of the people and the low level of production. Owing to both domestic circumstances and foreign influences, class struggle will continue to exist within a certain scope for a long time and may possibly grow acute under certain conditions, but it is no longer the principal contradiction. In building socialism, the basic task is to further release and develop the productive forces and achieve socialist modernization step by step by carrying out reform in those aspects and links of the production relations and the superstructure that do not conform to the development of the productive forces. The Party must uphold and improve the basic economic system, with public ownership playing a dominant role and different economic sectors developing side by side, as well as the system of distribution under which distribution according to work is dominant and a variety of modes of distribution coexist, encourage some areas and some people to become rich first, gradually eliminate poverty, achieve common prosperity, continuously meet the people's ever-growing material and cultural needs on the basis of the growth of production and social wealth and promote people's all-around development. Development is the Party's top priority in governing and rejuvenating the country. The general starting point and criterion for judging all the Party's work should be how it benefits development of the productive forces in China's socialist society, adds to the overall strength of socialist China and improves the people's living standards. The Party must respect work, knowledge, talent and creation and ensure that development is for the people, by the people and with the people sharing in its fruits. The beginning of the new century marks China's entry into the new stage of development of building a moderately prosperous society in all respects and accelerating socialist modernization. The Party must promote all-around economic, political, cultural, social, and ecological progress in accordance with the overall plan for the cause of socialism with Chinese characteristics. The strategic objectives of economic and social development at this new stage in the new century are to consolidate and develop the relatively comfortable life initially attained, bring China into a moderately prosperous society of a higher level to the benefit of well over one billion people by the time of the Party's centenary and bring the per capita GDP up to the level of moderately developed countries and realize modernization in the main by the time of the centenary of the People's Republic of China.

The basic line of the Communist Party of China in the primary stage of socialism is to lead the people of all ethnic

groups in a concerted, self-reliant and pioneering effort to turn China into a prosperous, strong, democratic, culturally advanced and harmonious modern socialist country by making economic development the central task while upholding the Four Cardinal Principles and the reform and opening up policy.

In leading the cause of socialism, the Communist Party of China must persist in taking economic development as the central task, making all other work subordinate to and serve this central task. The Party must lose no time in speeding up development, implement the strategy of rejuvenating the country through science and education, the strategy of strengthening the nation with trained personnel and the strategy of sustainable development, and give full play to the role of science and technology as the primary productive force. The Party must take advantage of the advancement of science and technology to improve the quality of workers and promote sound and rapid development of the national economy.

The Four Cardinal Principles – to keep to the socialist road and to uphold the people's democratic dictatorship, leadership by the Communist Party of China, and Marxism-Leninism and Mao Zedong Thought – are the foundation on which to build the country. Throughout the course of socialist modernization the Party must adhere to the Four Cardinal Principles and combat bourgeois liberalization.

Reform and opening up are the path to a stronger China. Only reform and opening up can enable China, socialism and Marxism to develop themselves. The Party must carry out fundamental reform of the economic structure that hampers the development of the productive forces, and keep to and improve the socialist market economy; it must also carry out corresponding political restructuring and reform in other fields. The Party must adhere to the basic state policy of opening up and assimilate and exploit the achievements of all other cultures. It must be bold in making explorations and breaking new ground in reform and opening up, make its reform decisions more scientific, better coordinate its reform measures and blaze new trails in practice.

The Communist Party of China leads the people in developing the socialist market economy. It unwaveringly consolidates and develops the public sector of the economy and unswervingly encourages, supports and guides the development of the non-public sector. It gives play to the basic role of market forces in allocating resources and works to set up a sound system of macroeconomic regulation. The Party works to balance urban and rural development, development among regions, economic and social development, relations between man and nature, and domestic development and opening to the outside world; adjust the economic structure, and transform the growth model. It is dedicated to promoting harmonized development of industrialization, IT application, urbanization and agricultural modernization, building a new socialist countryside, taking a new path of industrialization with Chinese characteristics, and making China an innovative country.

The Communist Party of China leads the people in **promoting socialist democracy.** It integrates its leadership, the position of the people as masters of the country, and the rule of law, takes the path of political development under socialism with Chinese characteristics, expands socialist democracy, improves the socialist legal system, builds a socialist country under the rule of law, consolidates the people's democratic dictatorship, and builds socialist political civilization. It upholds and improves the system of people's congresses, the system of multiparty cooperation and political consultation under its leadership, the system of regional ethnic autonomy, and the system of self-governance at the primary level of society. It makes people's democracy more extensive, fuller in scope and sounder in practice. It takes effective measures to protect the people's right to manage state and social affairs as well as economic and cultural programs. It respects and safeguards human rights. It encourages the free airing of views and works to establish sound systems and procedures of democratic election, decision-making, administration and oversight. It improves the socialist system of laws with Chinese characteristics and strengthens law enforcement, so as to bring all work of the state under the rule of law.

The Communist Party of China leads the people in **developing an advanced socialist culture.** It promotes socialist cultural and ethical progress, combines the rule of law and the rule of virtue in running the country and works to raise the ideological and moral standards and scientific and educational levels of the entire nation so as to provide a powerful ideological guarantee, motivation and intellectual support for reform, opening up and socialist modernization, and develop a strong socialist culture in China. It promotes core socialist values, adheres to Marxism as its guiding ideology, fosters the common ideal of socialism with Chinese characteristics, promotes patriotism-centered national spirit and the spirit of the times centering on reform and innovation and advocates the socialist maxims of honor and disgrace. It works to enhance the people's sense of national dignity, self-confidence and self-reliance, resist corrosion by decadent capitalist and feudal ideas and wipe out all social evils so that the people will have high ideals, moral integrity, a good education and a strong sense of discipline. It also needs to imbue its members with the lofty ideal of communism. The Party strives to develop educational, scientific and cultural programs, carry forward the fine traditional culture of the Chinese nation, and develop a thriving socialist culture.

The Communist Party of China leads the people in building **a harmonious socialist society.** In accordance with the general requirements for democracy and the rule of law, equity and justice, honesty and fraternity, vigor and vitality, stability and order, and harmony between man and nature and the principle of all the people building and sharing a harmonious socialist society, the Party focuses its efforts on ensuring and improving the people's wellbeing by solving the most specific problems of the utmost and immediate concern to the people, works to enable all the people to share in more fruits of development in a more equitable way, and strives to create a situation in which all people do their best, find their proper places in society and live together in harmony. The Party strengthens and makes innovations in social management. It strictly distinguishes between the two different types of contradictions – those between ourselves and the enemy and those among the people – and works to handle them correctly. It will strengthen comprehensive measures to maintain law and order, and resolutely combat criminal activities that endanger national security and interests, social stability and economic development and bring criminals to justice in accordance with the law, so as to maintain lasting social stability.

The Communist Party of China leads the people in **promoting socialist ecological progress.** It raises its ecological awareness of the need to respect, accommodate to and protect nature; follows the basic state policy of conserving resources and protecting the environment and the principle of giving high priority to conserving resources, protecting the environment and promoting its natural restoration; and pursues sound development that leads to increased production, affluence and a good ecosystem. The Party strives to build a resource-conserving, environmentally friendly society; and preserves China's geographical space and improves its industrial structure and mode of production and the Chinese way of life in the interest of conserving resources and protecting the environment. All this is aimed at creating a good working and living environment for the people and ensuring lasting and sustainable development of the Chinese nation.

The Communist Party of China persists in its **leadership over the People's Liberation Army** and other armed forces of the people, builds up the strength of the People's Liberation Army, ensures that it accomplishes its historic missions at this new stage in the new century, and gives full play to its role in consolidating national defense, defending the motherland and participating in the socialist modernization drive.

The Communist Party of China upholds and promotes **socialist ethnic relations based on equality, solidarity, mutual assistance and harmony,** actively trains and promotes cadres from among ethnic minorities, helps ethnic minorities and ethnic autonomous areas with their economic, cultural and social development, and ensures that all ethnic groups work together for common prosperity and development. The Party strives to fully implement its basic principle for its work related to religious affairs, and rallies religious believers in making contributions to economic and social development.

The Communist Party of China rallies all workers, farmers and intellectuals, and all the democratic parties, personages without party affiliation and the patriotic forces of all ethnic groups in China in further expanding and fortifying the **broadest possible patriotic united front** embracing all socialist workers, all builders of the cause of socialism and all patriots who support socialism or who support the reunification of the motherland. The Party will constantly strengthen the unity of all the Chinese people, including the compatriots in Hong Kong and Macao special administrative regions and in Taiwan as well as overseas Chinese. It will promote long-term prosperity and stability in Hong Kong and Macao and complete the great cause of reunifying the motherland in conformity with the principle of "one country, two systems."

The Communist Party of China adheres to an **independent foreign policy of peace,** follows the path of peaceful development and a win-win strategy of opening up, takes both the domestic and international situations into consideration, and vigorously develops relations with other countries in order to bring about a favorable international environment for China's reform, opening up and modernization. In international affairs, it safeguards China's independence and sovereignty, opposes hegemonism and power politics, defends world peace, promotes human progress, and pushes for the building of a harmonious world of lasting peace and common prosperity. It develops relations between China and other countries on the basis of the five principles of mutual respect for sovereignty and territorial integrity, mutual nonaggression, noninterference in each other's internal affairs, equality and mutual benefit, and peaceful coexistence. It strives for the constant development of good-neighborly relations between China and the surrounding countries and for the strengthening of the unity and cooperation between China and other developing countries. The Communist Party of China develops relations with communist parties and other political parties in other countries in accordance with the principles of independence, complete equality, mutual respect and noninterference in each other's internal affairs.

In order to lead the people of all ethnic groups in China in attaining the great goal of socialist modernization, the Communist Party of China must adhere to its basic line, strengthen its governance capability, advanced nature and purity and comprehensively carry forward the great new undertaking to build itself in a spirit of reform and innovation. The Party must make all-around efforts to strengthen itself ideologically and organizationally and improve its conduct; and it must become better able to combat corruption and uphold Party integrity and improve Party rules and regulations, thus making Party building more scientific in all respects. It must steadfastly build itself for public interests, exercise governance for the people, practice self-discipline, be strict with its members, and carry forward its fine traditions and style of work. It must constantly improve its art of leadership and governance, raise its ability to resist corruption, prevent degeneration and withstand risks, constantly strengthen its class foundation, expand its mass base and enhance its creativity, cohesion and combat effectiveness, and build itself into a learning, service-oriented and innovative Marxist governing party, so that it will stand forever in the forefront of the times and make itself a strong nucleus that can lead all the Chinese people in the unceasing march along the road of socialism with Chinese characteristics. In building itself, the Party must be determined to meet the following four essential requirements:

First, adhering to the Party's basic line. The whole Party must achieve unity in thinking and action with Deng Xiaoping Theory, the important thought of Three Represents, the Scientific Outlook on Development, and the Party's basic line, and persevere in doing so for a long time to come. The Party must integrate the reform and opening up policy with the Four Cardinal Principles, carry out its basic line in all fields of endeavor, implement in an all-around way its basic program for the primary stage of socialism and combat all "Left" and Right erroneous tendencies, maintaining vigilance against Right tendencies, primarily against "Left" tendencies. The Party must intensify the building of leading bodies at all levels, selecting and promoting cadres who have scored outstanding achievements in their public service and have won the trust of the masses in reform, opening up and the modernization drive, and train and cultivate millions upon millions of successors to the cause of socialism, thus ensuring organizationally the implementation of the Party's basic theory, line, program and experience.

Second, persevering in emancipating the mind, seeking truth from facts, keeping up with the times, and being realistic and pragmatic. The Party's ideological line is to proceed from reality in handling all matters, to integrate theory with practice, to seek truth from facts, and to verify and develop the truth through practice. All Party members must adhere to this ideological line, explore new ways, boldly experiment with new methods, go in for innovation, work creatively, constantly study new situations, review new experience and solve new problems, enrich and develop Marxism in practice, and advance the endeavor to adapt Marxism to Chinese conditions.

Third, persevering in serving the people wholeheartedly. The Party has no special interests of its own apart from the interests of the working class and the broadest masses of the people. At all times the Party gives top priority to the interests of the people, shares weal and woe with them, maintains the closest possible ties with them, and persists in exercising power for them, showing concern for them and working for their interests, and it does not allow any member to become divorced from the masses or place himself or herself above them. The Party follows the mass line in its work, doing everything for the masses, relying on them in every task, carrying out the principle of "from the masses, to the masses," and translating its correct views into action by the masses of their own accord. The biggest political advantage of the Party lies in its close ties with the masses while the biggest potential danger for it as a governing party comes from its divorce from them. The Party's style of work and its maintenance of ties with the masses of the people are a matter of vital importance to the Party. The Party will establish a sound system for punishing and preventing corruption by fighting it in a comprehensive way, addressing both its symptoms and root cause and combining punishment with prevention, with the emphasis on prevention. The Party will persistently oppose corruption and step up efforts to improve its style of work and uphold integrity.

Fourth, upholding democratic centralism. Democratic centralism is a combination of centralism on the basis of democracy and democracy under centralized guidance. It is the fundamental organizational principle of the Party and is also the mass line applied in the Party's political activities. The Party must fully expand intra-Party democracy, respect the principal position of its members, safeguard their democratic rights, and give play to the initiative and creativity of Party organizations at all levels as well as its members. Correct centralism must be practiced so as to ensure the solidarity, unity and concerted action in the whole Party and prompt and effective implementation of its decisions. The sense of organization and discipline must be strengthened, and all members are equal before Party discipline. Oversight of leading Party organs and of Party members holding leading positions, particularly principal leading cadres, must be strengthened and the system of intra-Party oversight constantly improved. In its internal political activities, the Party conducts criticism and self-criticism in the correct way, waging ideological struggles over matters of principle, upholding truth and rectifying mistakes. Diligent efforts must be made to create a political situation in which there are both centralism and democracy, both discipline and freedom, both unity of will and personal ease of mind and liveliness.

Leadership by the Party means mainly political, ideological and organizational leadership. The Party must meet the requirements of reform, opening up and socialist modernization, persist in scientific, democratic and law-based governance, and strengthen and improve its leadership. Acting on the principle that the Party commands the overall situation and coordinates the efforts of all quarters, the Party must play the role as the core of leadership among all other organizations at the corresponding levels. It must concentrate on leading economic development, organize and coordinate all forces in a concerted effort to focus on economic development and promote all-around economic and social development. The Party must practice democratic and scientific decision-making; formulate and implement the correct line, principles and policies; do its organizational, publicity and educational work well and make sure that all Party members play an exemplary and vanguard role. The Party must conduct its activities within the framework of the Constitution and laws of the country. It must see to it that the legislative, judicial and administrative organs of the state and the economic, cultural and people's organizations work with initiative and independent responsibility and in unison. The Party must strengthen its leadership over trade unions, the Communist Youth League, women's federations and other mass organizations, and give full scope to their roles. The Party must adapt itself to the march of events and changing circumstances, improving its system and style of leadership and raising its governance capability. Party members must work in close cooperation with non-Party persons in the common endeavor to build socialism with Chinese characteristics.

Source: http://www.chinadaily.com.cn/china/2012cpc/2012-11/21/content_15947761.htm

Revised and adopted at the 18th CPC Congress on November 14, 2012 (Emphasis added).

Index